BE SKILLFUL

Be Skillful

WARREN W. WIERSBE

Chariot VICTOR
PUBLISHING
A DIVISION OF COOK COMMUNICATIONS

Chariot Victor Publishing,
a division of Cook Communications, Colorado Springs, Colorado 80918
Cook Communications, Paris, Ontario
Kingsway Communications, Eastbourne, England

Cover Design: iDesignEtc.
Cover Photo: Faust Reynolds
Study Questions: Carol Smith

Library of Congress Cataloging-in-Publication Data
Wiersbe, Warren W.
    Be skillful / by Warren W. Wiersbe
        p. cm.
    Includes bibliographical references.
    ISBN 1-56476-430-3
    1. Bible O.T. Proverbs—Devotional literature
    2. Christian life—Biblical teaching. I. Title.
BS1465.4.W54   1995
223'.706—dc20   94-38286
                                          CIP

9 10 11   Printing/Year   03 02 01

CONTENTS

PREFACE

"Where is the wisdom we have lost in knowledge?" asked the late British poet T.S. Eliot. "Where is the knowledge we have lost in information?"[1]

We're living in the "information age," but we certainly aren't living in the "age of wisdom." Many people who are wizards with their computers seem to be amateurs when it comes to making a success out of their lives. Computers can store data and obey signals, but they can't give us the ability to use that knowledge wisely. What's needed today is wisdom.

The Book of Proverbs is about godly wisdom, how to get it and how to use it. It's about priorities and principles, not get-rich-quick schemes or success formulas. It tells you, not how to make a living, but how to be skillful in the lost art of making a life.

As you read, please keep your Bible before you and look up the many Bible references in these chapters. To skip over them is to miss some important truth; after all, what God has written is far more important than what I write! Also, read the endnotes. There's a good deal of helpful material in them that I couldn't include in the text. I don't want you to miss it.

As never before, the church desperately needs people who understand and practice the skills involved in building a godly life. May you and I be among them!

Warren W. Wiersbe

A Suggested Outline of the Book of Proverbs

Key Verse: Proverbs 1:7

Introduction: 1:1-19

ONE

INTRODUCTION
TO THE BOOK OF PROVERBS

Don't Just Make a Living —
Make a Life!

My wife, Betty, is the navigator in our household. For more than forty years, I've depended on her to plan our ministry trips and our occasional holidays and to direct me when I'm driving. She knows that I don't have a good sense of direction and have even been known to get lost just a few miles from home. But the Lord gave her built-in radar, and I've learned to trust her, whether we're in the big city, the African bush, or the English countryside.

I need a similar "spiritual radar" to guide me when I'm embarking on a "study journey" through a book of the Bible. That radar is provided by the Holy Spirit who guides us into God's truth (John 16:13) and, if we let Him, keeps us from going on unprofitable detours. But if I begin my journey by answering some basic questions about the book I'm studying, the Holy Spirit will find me better prepared for His teaching ministry. The questions I ask myself are:

(1) What is the major theme of the book?
(2) Who wrote the book and how is it written?
(3) What is the key verse that helps "unlock" the message of the book?

(4) What does this book say about Jesus Christ?

(5) What must I do to get the most out of this book?

Let's get prepared for our pilgrimage through Proverbs by answering these five questions.

1. What is the major theme of the Book of Proverbs? One word answers the question: *wisdom.* In Proverbs, the words *wise* and *wisdom* are used at least 125 times, because the aim of the book is to help us *acquire* and *apply* God's wisdom to the decisions and activities of daily life.

The Book of Proverbs belongs to what scholars call the "wisdom literature" of the Old Testament, which also includes Job and Ecclesiastes.[1] The writers of these books wrestled with some of the most difficult questions of life as they sought to understand life's problems from God's point of view. After all, just because you're a believer and you walk by faith, it doesn't mean you put your mind on the shelf and stop thinking. The Lord expects us to apply ourselves intellectually and do some serious thinking as we study His Word. We should love the Lord with our minds as well as with our hearts and souls (Matt. 22:37).

Wisdom was an important commodity in the ancient Near East; every ruler had his council of "wise men" whom he consulted when making important decisions. Joseph was considered a wise man in Egypt and Daniel and his friends were honored for their wisdom while serving in Babylon. God wants His children today to "walk circumspectly [carefully], not as fools but as wise" (Eph. 5:15, NKJV). Understanding the Book of Proverbs can help us do that. It isn't enough simply to be educated and have knowledge, as important as education is. We also need wisdom, which is the ability to use knowledge. Wise men and women have the competence to grasp the meaning of a situation and understand what to do and how to do it in the right way at the right time.

To the ancient Jew, wisdom was much more than simply good advice or successful planning. I like Dr. Roy Zuck's definition: "Wisdom means being skillful and successful in one's relationships and responsibilities . . . observing and following the Creator's principles of order in the moral universe."[2] In that definition you find most of the important elements of biblical wisdom, the kind of wisdom we can learn from the Book of Proverbs.

Biblical wisdom begins with a right relationship with the Lord. The wise person believes that there is a God, that He is the Creator and Ruler of all things, and that He has put within His creation a divine order that, if obeyed, leads ultimately to success. Wise people also assert that there is a moral law operating in this world, a principle of divine justice which makes sure that eventually the wicked are judged and the righteous are rewarded. Biblical wisdom has little if any relationship to a person's IQ or education, because it is a matter of moral and spiritual understanding. It has to do with character and values; it means looking at the world through the grid of God's truth.

In the Old Testament, the Hebrew word for "wise" *(hakam)* is used to describe people skillful in working with their hands, such as the artisans who helped build the tabernacle (Ex. 28:3; 35:30—36:2) and Solomon's temple (1 Chron. 22:15). Wisdom isn't something theoretical, it's something very practical that affects every area of life. It gives order and purpose to life it gives discernment in making decisions; and it provides a sense of fulfillment in life to the glory of God.

Wisdom keeps us in harmony with the principles and purposes that the Lord has built into His world so that as we obey God, everything works for us and not against us. This doesn't mean we don't experience trials and difficulties, because trials and difficulties are a normal part of life. But it means we have the ability to deal with these adversities successfully so that we grow spiritually and the Lord is glorified.

People with wisdom have the skill to face life honestly and courageously, and to manage it successfully so that God's purposes are fulfilled in their lives. That's why I've called this book *Be Skillful,* because we're seeking to learn from Proverbs the divine principles that can make us skillful, not in making a living, but in making a life. The pages of history are filled with the names of brilliant and gifted people who were *smart* enough to become rich and famous but not *wise* enough to make a successful and satisfying life. Before his death, one of the world's richest men said that he would have given all his wealth to make one of his six marriages succeed. It's one thing to make a living, but quite something else to make a life.

2. Who wrote the Book of Proverbs and how is it written?
Author. In 1:1, 10:1, and 25:1, we're told that King Solomon is the author of the proverbs in this book. God gave Solomon great wisdom (1 Kings 3:5-15), so that people came from the ends of the earth to listen to him and returned home amazed (4:29-34; Matt. 12:42). He spoke 3,000 proverbs, most of which are not included in this book. The Holy Spirit selected only those proverbs that the people of God should understand and obey in every age.[3]

But other servants, guided by God's Spirit, were also involved in producing this book. "The men of Hezekiah" (Prov. 25:1) were a group of scholars in King Hezekiah's day (700 B.C.) who compiled the material recorded in chapters 25–29, and in Proverbs 30 and 31, you meet "Agur the son of Jakeh" and "King Lemuel," although many scholars think "Lemuel" was another name for Solomon. Most of the material in this book came from King Solomon, so it's rightly called "the proverbs of Solomon" (1:1).

12

As every Bible reader knows, Solomon began his reign as a man of wisdom but ended his life practicing the greatest folly (1 Kings 11; Deut. 17:14-20). In order to achieve his political goals and keep the kingdom in peace, Solomon allied himself to other nations by marrying hundreds of women, and these heathen princesses gradually turned his heart away from loyalty to the Lord. How tragic that Solomon didn't even obey the precepts he wrote in his own book!

Approach. "Always do right—this will gratify some and astonish the rest." Mark Twain said that, and President Harry S. Truman liked the quotation so much he had it framed and placed on the wall behind his desk in the Oval Office.

Whether or not they tell the whole truth, clever sayings like Twain's are like burrs that stick in your mind. You find yourself recalling them and quoting them. This is especially true of proverbs, some of which are now so ancient they've become clichés. I once had to tell a pastor that my schedule wouldn't allow me to accept his kind invitation to speak at his church. He replied, "Oh, well, nothing ventured, nothing gained." The proverb he quoted has been around a long time. Chaucer quoted a version of it in one of his poems—in 1385!

Almost every tribe and nation has its share of proverbs expressed in ways that make it easy to "hang" proverbial wisdom in the picture gallery of your memory. "Every invalid is a physician," says an Irish proverb, and a Serbian proverb reads, "If vinegar is free, it is sweeter than honey." A proverb from Crete is a favorite of mine: "When you want a drink of milk, you don't buy the whole cow." Centuries ago, the Romans smiled at timid politicians and soldiers and said to each other, "The cat would eat fish, but she doesn't want to get her feet wet."

As an intellectual exercise, I challenge you to expand those four proverbs into four paragraphs of explanation. If you do, you'll learn to appreciate the brevity and richness of good proverbs. Proverbs are pithy statements that summarize in a few choice words practical truths relating to some aspect of everyday life. The Spanish novelist Cervantes defined a proverb as "a short sentence based on long experience." From a literary point of view, that isn't a bad definition.

Some people think that our English word *proverb* comes from the Latin *proverbium,* which means "a set of words put forth," or, "a saying supporting a point." Or, it may come from the Latin *pro* ("instead of," "on behalf of") and *verba* ("words"); that is, a short statement that takes the place of many words. The proverb "Short reckonings make long friendships" comes across with more power than a lecture on forgiving your friends. One of my junior high school teachers, when she heard the low murmur of pupils talking in class, would say, "Empty barrels make the most noise," and that would take care of the problem.

The Hebrew word *mashal* is translated "proverb," "parable," and even "allegory," but its basic meaning is "a comparison." Many of Solomon's proverbs are comparisons or contrasts (see 11:22; 25:25; 26:6-9), and some of his proverbs present these comparisons by using the word "better" (see 15:16-17; 16:19, 32; 17:1; 19:1).

Throughout the centuries, familiar maxims and proverbial sayings have been compiled into books, but no collection is more important than the Old Testament Book of Proverbs. For one thing, the Book of Proverbs is a part of Scripture and therefore is inspired by the Spirit of God (2 Tim. 3:16-17). Proverbs contains much more than clever sayings based on man's investigation and interpretation of human experience. Because God inspired this book, it is a part of divine revelation and relates the concerns of human life to God and the eternal. The Book of Proverbs is quoted in the New Testament[4] and therefore has a practical application to the lives of believers today.

According to 2 Timothy 3:16-17, "All Scripture is . . . profitable" in four ways: for *doctrine* — that's what's right; for *reproof* — that's what's not right; for *correction* — that's how to get right; and for *instruction in righteousness* — that's how to stay right. You will find all four of these purposes fulfilled in the Book of Proverbs. These inspired sayings teach us about God, man, sin, creation, and a host of other doctrinal topics. These proverbs rebuke and reprove sinners for their lying, laziness, drunkenness, sexual sins, and other personal failures. But Proverbs doesn't stop with conviction; the book also administers correction, telling us how to turn from sin and mend our ways. It shows us how to stay on the path of wisdom and not stray again.

My friend Dr. Bob Cook, now home with the Lord, told me that he started reading Proverbs regularly when he was just a boy. There are thirty-one chapters in Proverbs, so if you read a chapter a day, you can read the book through once a month. Bob's father promised to give him a dollar every time he faithfully finished reading the book, so every year Bob gained spiritual treasure and earned twelve dollars just by reading Proverbs.

Traditional man-made proverbs don't always agree with each other and aren't always right, but you can trust the Book of Proverbs. "Look before you leap" advises caution, while, "He who hesitates is lost" warns you not to miss your golden opportunity. Which maxim do you follow? "Many hands make light work" is contradicted by, "Too many cooks spoil the broth." However, the proverbs in Scripture are consistent with each other and with the total pattern of divine truth given in the Bible. Furthermore, the children of God have the Holy Spirit to guide them as they seek for God's wisdom in God's Word, because the Holy Spirit is "the Spirit of wisdom" (Isa. 11:2; Eph. 1:17).

But we still have to answer the important question, "Why

did Solomon use proverbs and not some other kind of literary approach as he recorded these divine truths?" Keep in mind that, apart from kings, prophets, and priests, the average Jewish adult didn't own copies of their sacred books and had to depend on memory to be able to meditate on God's truth and discuss it (Deut. 6:1-9). If Solomon had written a lecture on pride, few people would remember it, so he wrote a proverb instead: "Pride goes before destruction, a haughty spirit before a fall" (Prov. 16:18, NIV). There are only seven words in the original Hebrew, and even a child could memorize seven words!

Because proverbs are brief and pictorial, they are easy to memorize, recall, and share. Edward Everett's two-hour oration at the Gettysburg battlefield is written in American history books, but Abraham Lincoln's two-minute "Gettysburg Address" is written on the hearts of millions of people. Believers who learn the key proverbs in this book will have at their disposal the wisdom they need for making right decisions day after day. The truths found in Proverbs touch upon every important area of human life, such as acquiring and using wealth, making and keeping friends, building a happy home, avoiding temptation and trouble, controlling our feelings, disciplining the tongue, and building godly character.

Analysis. But why didn't the Holy Spirit direct the authors to arrange these proverbs in topical fashion, so we could quickly find what we need to know? Derek Kidner reminds us that the Book of Proverbs, "is no anthology, but a course of education in the life of wisdom."[5] As we read Proverbs chapter by chapter, the Spirit of God has the freedom to teach us about many subjects, and we never know from day to day which topic we'll need the most. Just as the Bible itself isn't arranged like a systematic theology, neither is Proverbs. What Solomon wrote is more like a kaleidoscope than a stained-glass window: We never know what the next pattern will be.

The first nine chapters of Proverbs form a unit in which the emphasis is on "wisdom" and "folly," personified as two women. (The Hebrew word for wisdom is in the feminine gender.) In chapters 1, 8, and 9, Wisdom calls to men and women to follow her and enjoy salvation, wealth,[6] and life. In chapters 5, 6, and 7, Folly calls to the same people and offers them immediate satisfaction, but doesn't warn them of the tragic consequences of rejecting Wisdom: condemnation, poverty, and death. Chapters 10–15 form the next unit and present a series of *contrasts* between the life of wisdom and the life of folly. The closing chapters of the book (16–31) contain a variety of proverbs that give us *counsel* about many important areas of life.

As you survey Solomon's approach, you can see how wise God was in arranging the book this way. Wisdom isn't some abstract treasure that's so far away we can't grasp it. Through His Word and by His Spirit, God is every day calling us to the life of wisdom. If we want to live wisely, *we must begin with commitment to Jesus Christ,* who is "the wisdom of God" (1 Cor. 1:30). Wisdom and Folly each want to control our lives, and we must make the choice.

After we have committed ourselves to the Lord and His wisdom, we must recognize that there are consequences to the decisions we make. The proverbs in chapters 10–15 depict so vividly the contrasts that exist between the life of wisdom and the life of folly, between faith and unbelief, obedience and disobedience. We can't compromise and expect God to bless. The final section of the book (chaps. 16–31) contains the further counsels we need for developing spiritual discernment and making wise decisions.

3. What is the key verse that helps "unlock" the book?
I suggest that 1:7 is the key verse we're looking for: "The fear of the Lord is the beginning [chief part] of knowledge:

17

but fools despise wisdom and instruction." This statement is amplified in 9:10—"The fear of the Lord is the beginning of wisdom: and the knowledge of the holy [Holy One] is understanding." See also Job 28:28 and Psalm 111:10.

There are at least eighteen references to "the fear of the Lord" in Proverbs (1:7, 29; 2:5; 3:7; 8:13; 9:10; 10:27; 14:2, 26-27; 15:16, 33; 16:6; 19:23; 22:4; 23:17; 24:21; 31:30). If you read all these verses carefully, you'll get a good idea of what this important biblical phrase means.

If we truly "fear the Lord," we acknowledge from our hearts that He's the Creator, we're the creatures; He's the Father, we're His children; He's the Master, we're the servants. It means to respect God for who He is, to listen carefully to what He says, and to obey His Word, knowing that our disobedience displeases Him, breaks our fellowship with Him, and invites His chastening. It's not the servile fear of the slave before the master but the reverential and respectful fear of the child before the parent. Children fear not only because their parents can hurt them, but also because *they can hurt their parents*. Proverbs 13:13 admonishes us to fear God's commandments, which suggests that the way we treat our Bible is the way we treat God.

"But what is this fear of the Lord?" asks Charles Bridges, and he answers the question adequately: "It is that affectionate reverence by which the child of God bends himself humbly and carefully to his Father's law. His wrath is so bitter, and His love so sweet; that hence springs an earnest desire to please Him, and—because of the danger of coming short from his own weakness and temptations—a holy watchfulness and *fear,* 'that he might not sin against Him.' "[7]

The six verses that precede this key verse (1:7) explain why the Book of Proverbs was written: to give us wisdom, instruction, understanding, subtlety (prudence), knowledge, discretion, learning, and counsel. Everything depends on wisdom; the other seven words are practically synonymous with it.

Louis Goldberg says that wisdom means exhibiting "His [God's] character in the many practical affairs of life."[8] *Instruction* carries the idea of discipline, a parent's correction that results in the building of the child's character. *Understanding* means the ability to grasp a truth with insight and discernment. *Prudence* ("subtlety") is the kind of intelligence that sees the reasons behind things. People with prudence can think their way through complex matters and see what lies behind them, and thereby make wise decisions about them. (In a negative sense, the word translated "prudence" means craftiness. It is used to describe Satan in Gen. 3:1.)

The word translated *knowledge* comes from a Hebrew root that describes skill in hunting (Gen. 25:27), sailing (2 Chron. 8:18), and playing a musical instrument (1 Sam. 16:16). Knowledge involves the ability to distinguish; the Latin equivalent gives us our English word *science*. *Discretion* is the ability to devise wise plans after understanding a matter. The negative meaning is "to devise a plot."

The Hebrew root for *learning* means "to lay hold of, to grasp, to acquire or buy." When we grasp something with the mind, then we have learned it. The word translated *counsel* is related to the verb "to steer a ship." Counsel is wise guidance that moves one's life in the right direction.

You'll find these eight words repeated often in the Book of Proverbs; when you put them together, you have a summary of what Solomon means by wisdom.

4. What does Proverbs say about Jesus Christ?

In Jesus Christ "are hid all the treasures of wisdom and knowledge" (Col. 2:3), and He is our wisdom (1 Cor. 1:24, 30). Solomon was the wisest ruler who ever lived, and yet Jesus Christ is "greater than Solomon" in both His wisdom and His wealth (Matt. 12:42). Certainly all the beautiful qualities of wisdom described in Proverbs are seen in Jesus Christ, and His earthly walk is a pattern for God's people to follow (1 John 2:6).

The description of wisdom in Proverbs 8:22-31 suggests Jesus Christ as the eternal wisdom of God, but that isn't the main thrust of the passage. Solomon personifies wisdom as the joyful son of a father, a master craftsman, and reminds us that wisdom is one of God's eternal attributes. God magnified His wisdom in the way He created the universe. The "laws of nature" that form the basis for modern science were "built into" the universe by the wisdom of God. When we honestly study creation, no matter what branch of science we follow, we're only thinking God's thoughts after Him. Jesus Christ, the eternal creative Word, was there in the beginning (John 1:1-5; Heb. 1:1-4; Col. 1:15-17).[9] Wise people learn the eternal "wise principles" of life built into creation and seek to obey them.

5. What must we do to get the most out of this book? Solomon often uses the phrase, "my son" (Prov. 1:8, 10, 15; 2:1; 3:1, 11, 21; 4:10, 20; 5:1, 20; 6:1, 3, 20; 7:1; 19:27; 23:15, 19, 26; 24:13, 21; 27:11), which suggests that Proverbs contains truths that loving godly parents would pass along to their children[10] (see 1 Chron. 29:1). As God's children, we need His loving counsel, and He gives it to us in this book. So, the first essential for an effective study of Proverbs is *faith in Jesus Christ so that you can honestly call God your Father.* You can't *make* a life until you first *have* life, and this life comes through faith in Jesus Christ (John 3:16, 36).

What applies to the study of Proverbs applies to the study of any book in the Bible: Unless we are spiritually prepared, diligent, disciplined in study, and obedient to what God tells us, we won't really understand very much of God's Word. A willingness to obey is essential (John 7:17). F.W. Robertson said that, "obedience is the organ of spiritual knowledge." The Holy Spirit teaches the serious, not the curious.

At least a dozen times in Proverbs you find the imperatives "hear" or "hearken"[11] (Prov. 1:8; 4:1, 10; 5:7; 7:24; 8:6, 32-33; 19:20; 22:17; 23:19, 22); many other verses explain the blessings that come to those who obey (who hear and heed) the Word of God (1:5, 33; 8:34; 12:15; 15:31-32). In fact, Solomon warns us not to listen to instruction that will lead us astray (19:27; see Ps. 1:1). This doesn't mean that Christian students can't study the classics and books written by nonbelievers, but they must be careful to read them in the light of the Scriptures. The counsel of godly Robert Murray M'Cheyne is helpful: "Beware the atmosphere of the classics," he wrote to a friend in college. "True, we ought to know them; but only as chemists handle poisons — to discover their qualities, not to infect their blood with them."[12]

As you study, keep in mind that Hebrew proverbs are generalized statements of what is usually true in life, and they must not be treated like promises. "A friend loves at all times" (Prov. 17:17, NKJV), but sometimes even the most devoted friends may have disagreements. "A soft answer turns away wrath" (15:1, NKJV) in most instances, but our Lord's lamblike gentleness didn't deliver Him from shame and suffering. The assurance of life for the obedient is given often (3:2, 22; 4:10, 22; 8:35; 9:11; 10:27; 12:28; 13:14; 14:27; 19:23; 21:21; 22:4) and generally speaking, this is true. Obedient believers will care for their bodies and minds and avoid substances and practices that destroy, but some godly saints have died very young while more than one godless rebel has had a long life. David Brainerd, missionary to the American Indians, died at thirty. Robert Murray M'Cheyne died just two months short of his thirtieth birthday. Henry Martyn, missionary to India and Persia, died at thirty-two. William

Whiting Borden, who gave his fortune to God's work, was only twenty-five years old when he died in Egypt on his way to China.

"The righteous man is rescued from trouble, and it comes on the wicked instead" (11:8, NIV) certainly happened to Mordecai (Es. 7) and Daniel (Dan. 6), but millions of Christian martyrs testify to the fact that the statement isn't an absolute in this life. In fact, in Psalm 73, Asaph concludes that the wicked get the upper hand in this world, but the godly have their reward for eternity. The Book of Proverbs has little to say about the life to come; it focuses on this present life and gives guidelines for making wise decisions that help to produce a satisfying life.

God calls us to receive His wisdom and be skillful, so that we can make a life that will glorify Him. The important thing isn't how long we live but how we live, not the length but the depth of life. Fools wade in the shallows, but wise people launch out into the deep and let God give them His very best.

TWO

Is Anybody Listening?

Three hundred years before Christ, the Greek philosopher Zeno made a statement that he never dreamed would become a powerful weapon for parents everywhere. No doubt your parents quoted Zeno's words to you whenever as a child you talked too much: "The reason why we have two ears and only one mouth is that we may listen the more and talk the less."

If ancient Greece had been as noisy as our world today, Zeno might have changed his mind and covered his ears. The Greeks didn't have the necessities of life that we have, like radios and televisions (both stationary and portable), amplified rock music (120 decibels), telephones and pesky solicitation calls, movies, camcorders and VCRs, and all the other devices that have invaded modern life. Zeno never heard a jet plane (140 decibels) or a power mower (100 decibels), nor did he ever stop his car next to a vehicle inhabited by sinister stereo speakers emitting sounds so loud that the vehicle was shaking. Zeno never spent the night in a motel room with tissue paper walls separating him from the room next door where a TV set was being ignored by a guest who was obviously deaf.

"Listen more and talk less." Bah, humbug! There are times when about the only way you can protect your sanity and your hearing is to open your mouth and say something, even if it's only a primal scream.

But the greatest tragedy of life isn't that people invade our privacy, get on our nerves, and help destroy our delicate hearing apparatus. The greatest tragedy is that there's so much noise that *people can't hear the things they really need to hear.* God is trying to get through to them with the voice of wisdom, but all they hear are the confused communications clutter, foolish voices that lead them farther away from the truth. Even without our modern electronic noisemakers, a similar situation existed in ancient Israel when Solomon wrote Proverbs, because there's really nothing new under the sun. God was speaking to people in Solomon's day, but they weren't listening.

If you'll refer to the suggested outline of Proverbs, you'll see that the first nine chapters present two women — Wisdom and Folly personified — as they seek to win the attention and obedience of people in the city streets and squares. In this chapter, I want to focus on Wisdom's calls, and then in the next chapter we'll listen to Folly and learn what she has to offer.

1. Wisdom's call to salvation (Prov. 1:8-33)

This paragraph records three voices that the person reading Proverbs needs to identify.

The voice of instruction (vv. 8-10, 15-19). This is the voice of a godly father, urging his son to listen to Wisdom and obey what he hears. Note that both the father and the mother have been involved in teaching the boy,[1] and they both warn him not to abandon what he's been told. These parents have obeyed the instructions of Moses (Deut. 6:6-9) and have faithfully taught their family the Word of God. But what will

24

their children do with all this teaching?

The parents' desire is that the children obey what they have learned, so that God's truth will become a lovely ornament to beautify their lives, like a crown on a king or a necklace on a queen. Paul told Christian servants to "adorn the doctrine of God our Savior in all things" (Titus 2:10), which simply means to make the Bible beautiful to others by living a godly life. Peter exhorted Christian wives to win their lost husbands by focusing on the imperishable beauty of Christian character rather than the artificial beauty of man-made glamour (1 Peter 3:3-4).

In Proverbs 1:15-19, the father tells his son how to avoid yielding to temptation. First, he says, check carefully the path you're on and don't walk with the wrong crowd. (This sounds very much like Ps. 1:1 and 2 Cor. 6:14-18.) If you're walking with the wrong crowd, you'll end up doing the wrong things. Second, don't play with temptation, because temptation always leads to a trap (Prov. 1:17). Birds don't take bait when they can plainly see the trap, and people ought to be smarter than birds.[2]

Third, when you disobey God by harming others, you only harm yourself (vv. 18-19). You're free to take what you want from life, but eventually you'll have to pay for it, and the price you pay is higher than the value you gain. You end up sacrificing the permanent for the immediate, and that's a bad investment.

The voice of temptation (vv. 11-14). Anybody who makes it easy for us to disobey God certainly isn't a friend. The offer they made sounded exciting, but it only led to disaster. How tragic that a group of people would actually find enjoyment in doing evil, and how foolish of them to think their loot would satisfy their desires. They rejected the eternal treasures of wisdom (3:14-16; 16:16) for the cheap trinkets of this world, and they lost their souls in the bargain.

The voice of salvation (vv. 20-33). How does Wisdom speak? In a loud ringing voice that everybody can hear! Through both creation (Rom. 10:18; Ps. 19:1-4) and conscience (Rom. 2:14-16), "what may be known of God is manifest in them [the lost world], for God has shown it to them" (Rom. 1:19, NKJV). The church's task is to proclaim the Gospel message so everybody can hear, believe, and be saved. Like Wisdom, we must herald the Word in an uncompromising way.

Where does Wisdom speak? In the crowded streets and public places where busy people gather to take care of the business of life. The message of God's truth is made for the marketplace, not the ivory tower; we must share it "at the head of the noisy streets" (Prov. 1:21, NIV). Wisdom even went to the city gate where the leaders were transacting official business. No matter where people are, they need to hear Wisdom's call.

To whom does Wisdom speak? To three classes of sinners: the simple ones, the scorners (scoffers, mockers, NIV), and the fools[3] (v. 22). The *simple* are naive people who believe anything (14:15) but examine nothing. They're gullible and easily led astray. *Scorners* think they know everything (21:24) and laugh at the things that are really important. While the simple one has a blank look on his face, the scorner wears a sneer. *Fools* are people who are ignorant of truth because they're dull and stubborn. Their problem isn't a low IQ or poor education; their problem is a lack of spiritual desire to seek and find God's wisdom. Fools enjoy their foolishness but don't know how foolish they are! The outlook of fools is purely materialistic and humanistic. They hate knowledge and have no interest in things eternal. I'll have more to say about each of these in a later chapter.

What does wisdom say to them? First, she brings an *indictment* against them (1:22) and asks how long they plan to remain in their dangerous spiritual condition. Wisdom has spoken to them time and time again, but they have refused to listen, and this will make their judgment even more severe. Then Wisdom issues an *invitation* that they turn from their evil ways and receive her gifts (v. 23). This is a call to repentance and faith. She promises to change their hearts and teach them the wisdom of God from the Word of God.

How do the simple, the scorners, and the fools respond to Wisdom? They refuse to obey her voice; they won't take hold of her outstretched hand; they laugh at her warnings; and they mock her words. Note the word "also" in verse 26. Because they laughed at Wisdom, one day Wisdom will also laugh at them. Because they mocked her, she will mock them. Wisdom sees a storm of judgment coming that will bring distress and anguish to all who reject God's invitation.

When that judgment arrives, sinners will call upon the Lord but it will be too late. "Seek the Lord while He may be found, call upon Him while He is near" (Isa. 55:6, NKJV). Sinners will reap what they have sown. "Therefore they shall eat the fruit of their own way, and be filled to the full with their own fancies" (Prov. 1:31, NKJV). They turned away their ears from hearing the truth (v. 32; see 2 Tim. 4:4) and were complacently comfortable with believing lies. In contrast to the judgment promised to unbelievers, wisdom promises security and peace to those who will listen to her and believe (Prov. 1:33).

2. Wisdom's call to true wealth (Prov. 8:1-36)

In His mercy, the Lord continues to call to sinners because He is "long-suffering toward us, not willing that any should perish but that all should come to repentance" (2 Peter 3:9, NKJV). Wisdom returns to the crowded places of the city and calls out so everyone may hear. But note that she addresses the simple and the fools *but not the scorners* (compare Prov. 1:22 with 8:5). They had laughed at her message and turned away from the truth, so their opportunities were over, not because God wasn't speaking but because their hearts were too hard to hear. "Today, if you will hear His voice, do not harden your hearts" (Heb. 4:7-8, NKJV). "See that you do not refuse Him who speaks" (12:25, NKJV).

Wisdom's second message has three very clear points, followed by a call to decision.

"You can trust my words" (vv. 6-9). Five adjectives are used here to describe the character of the message Wisdom declares. Her words are "excellent" (v. 6), a word that is often translated "captain" or "ruler" in the Old Testament. The NIV reads "worthy things," and other translations use "noble" or "princely." Since God's message is the Word of the King, it is indeed noble and princely.

The message also contains "right things" (vv. 6, 9), a word that describes something straight. The English word "right" comes from the Latin *rectus* which means "straight." This root is also seen in words like "direct" and "correct." God's Word is also true (v. 7) and righteous (v. 8). Folly uses deceptive and "crooked" words to achieve her purposes, language that George Orwell called "newspeak" in his novel *Nineteen Eighty-Four* and that we would today call "double-speak." Whatever God's Word says about anything is right and can be trusted (Ps. 119:128). "The judgments of the Lord are true and righteous altogether" (19:9, NKJV).

Wisdom's words are plain, spoken clearly and openly so that there can be no confusion. Of course, those who reject the Lord don't understand what God is saying (1 Cor. 2:12-16), but this isn't because the Word of God is confusing or unclear. It's because sinners are spiritually blind and deaf (Matt. 13:14-15). The problem is with the hearer, not the speaker. Mark Twain is supposed to have said, "It isn't what I don't understand about the Bible that worries me, but what I do understand."

"You can receive true wealth" (vv. 10-21). This passage deals with enrichment, not riches in the material sense. Wisdom isn't promising to put money in the bank for us; she's urging us to seek eternal wealth instead of gold, silver, and precious stones (see vv. 18-19 as well as 2:4; 3:13-15 and 1 Cor. 3:12) This is an Old Testament version of Matthew 6:33: "But seek first the kingdom of God and His righteousness, and all these things shall be added to you" (NKJV).

Some Israelites during the Old Testament era had the idea that wealth was a sign of God's blessing while poverty and trouble were evidences that you were out of His favor. Because Job's friends held to a "prosperity theology," they concluded that Job was a great sinner or he wouldn't be suffering so much. When Jesus said it was hard for a rich man to enter God's kingdom, His astounded disciples asked, "Who then can be saved?" (Matt. 19:23-26) If rich people don't make it to heaven, who will?

But Wisdom has better gifts to offer than perishable riches — blessings like prudence, knowledge, discretion ("witty inventions," Prov. 8:12), the fear of the Lord, humility, godly speech, wise counsel, understanding, guidance on life's path, strength for the journey, and "durable riches." A life that's enriched by God may be poor in this world's goods, but it is rich in the things that matter most. It's good to enjoy the things that money can buy, provided you don't lose the things that money can't buy. *What Wisdom has to offer can't be purchased anywhere, no matter how rich you are.*

How do we secure this satisfying and enduring wealth? Hear the Word of God (v. 6), receive instruction (v. 10), love truth and wisdom (vv. 17, 21), and seek God and His wisdom daily (v. 17). Many of God's people have discovered how important it is to start each day with the Lord, meditating on His Word, praying and worshiping Him. See Psalms 57:8 and 63:11; Genesis 19:27; Exodus 24:4; and Mark 1:35.

"You can see My works" *(vv. 22-31).* We touched upon this in chapter 1 and found it to be an explanation of the wisdom of God at work in the creation of the universe. While it isn't a description of Jesus Christ, for the eternal Son of God was never created, it does foreshadow Christ as the creative Word that brought everything into being (John 1:1-4; Col. 2:3).

One of the lessons of this paragraph is that the power and splendor of God, seen all around us in creation, are evidence of what God's wisdom can do. The same God who worked in the "old creation" also wants to work in our lives in the "new creation" (2 Cor. 5:17; Eph. 2:10; 4:24; Col. 3:10). The Lord Jesus Christ, who holds the universe together and causes it to fulfill His will, can hold our lives together and accomplish His purposes for His glory.

When we belong to Jesus Christ and walk in His wisdom, all of creation works for us; if we rebel against His wisdom and will, things start to work against us, as Jonah discovered when he tried to run away from the Lord.

"You must make a decision!" *(vv. 32-36)* Having declared God's truth, Wisdom now calls for a decision, as all faithful heralds must do. How people respond to God's message is a matter of life or death (vv. 35-36), and it's impossible to be neutral. Wisdom calls for a sincere life-changing decision that involves turning from sin (repentance) and turning to Christ (faith). If the decision is real, it will result in a commitment to the Lord that leads to meeting with Him daily, like a servant at the master's door.

Those who reject God's truth sin against their own souls. Those who hate God's truth are heading for eternal death (Rev. 20:11-15).

3. Wisdom's call to life (Prov. 9:1-18)

Instead of going to the busy places of the city, Wisdom now remains at home and serves as hostess of a grand feast.

Preparation (vv. 1-2). In the previous chapter, we saw Wisdom at work in creation, but here we see her having built a spacious house ("seven pillars") where she prepares a sumptuous banquet. The Jewish people didn't use their flocks and herds for food, so opportunities to eat roast beef or lamb were infrequent and welcomed. The table would be spread with delectable foods as well as wine to drink. "Mingled" (mixed) wine could mean diluted with water (usually three parts water) or mixed with spices. However, the presence of wine on the table must not be interpreted as a divine endorsement of alcoholic beverages. Wine was a normal part of a Jewish meal, but nowhere does the Bible approve of drunkenness (see 20:1; 23:29-35; 31:4-7). More on this topic in a later chapter.

Invitation (vv. 3-9). Instead of going out herself as in the previous two "calls," Wisdom now sends her lovely maidens to the highest places of the city to invite people to the feast. It was customary in those times for a host or hostess to issue two invitations. The first one, given some days in advance, notified the guests of the day and hour of the feast; the second one, given the day of the feast, ascertained who was actually coming (see Luke 14:16-24; Matt. 22:1-14). Knowing the approximate number of the guests, the cooks could then prepare sufficient meat so that there was plenty for everybody and nothing would be wasted. We don't read here of any preliminary invitation. The maidens are simply saying, "Come right now!"

Note that they are inviting one class of people: the simple (Prov. 9:4). Wisdom's first call was to the simple, the scorners, and the fools (1:22). The scorners laughed at her, so in her second call she invited only the simple and the fools (8:5). But the fools didn't want God's wisdom, so in this third call she invites only the simple ones to come to her feast. It's a dangerous thing to reject God's invitation; you never know when it may be your last one (Luke 14:24).

Of course, when the simple people accept the invitation, it means leaving the old crowd, and the fools and scoffers will try to talk them into staying (Prov. 9:6-8). Sinners don't want to be rebuked and reproved, but wise people will accept and benefit from both. Fools, scoffers, and the simple like to have their own way and be told they're doing fine, but wise men and women want the truth. Teach wise people and they'll accept the truth and become wiser; try to teach fools and they'll reject the truth and become even greater fools.

Celebration (vv. 10-12). When you respond to Wisdom's invitation and attend the feast, what will you receive? For one thing, you'll have a greater respect for the Lord and a deeper knowledge of the Holy One (v. 10). The better you know God, the keener will be your knowledge and discernment when it comes to the decisions of life.

Once again, Wisdom promises to give us long life (v. 11) and to fill our days and years with rich experiences of God's grace. God wants to add years to our life and life to our years, and He will do it if we obey His wisdom. Verse 12 reminds us that the Lord wants to build godly character into our lives, and we can't borrow character from others or give our character to them. This is an individual matter that involves individual decisions. Belonging to a fine family, attending a faithful church, or studying in an excellent school can't guarantee the building of our character. Character is built on decisions, and bad decisions will create bad character.

Condemnation (vv. 13-18). The chapter closes with a quick glimpse of the prostitute (Folly) as she calls to the same simple ones and invites them to her house. But if they accept her invitation, they'll be attending a funeral and not a feast — and it will be their own funeral!

In 5:15-18, Solomon compared the joys of married love to drinking pure water from a refreshing fountain, but Folly (the adulteress) offers "stolen water" from somebody else's fountain. God ordained marriage to be a "fence" around the fountain so that nobody will pollute it. "Thou shalt not commit adultery" (Ex. 20:14) has never been removed from God's Law.

When it comes to possessing eternal life and living so as to please God, it's an either/or situation. Either we accept the invitation or we reject it; either we obey His wisdom or we reject it. Those who claim to be neutral are rejecting His Word as much as those who turn away from it completely. "He that is not with Me is against Me," said Jesus (Matt. 12:30).

What will it be in your life, the feast or the funeral?

THREE

The Path of Wisdom and Life

A newspaper cartoon shows an automobile balancing precariously over the edge of a cliff, with an embarrassed husband at the wheel and his disgusted wife sitting next to him. Meekly, he says to his wife, "Honey, there's got to be a lesson here somewhere."

There's a lesson there all right, and it's this: *The only way to end up at the right destination is to choose the right road.* If you've ever made a wrong turn in a strange place and found yourself lost, then you know how important that lesson is.

The metaphor of life as a journey is a familiar one; it is found in the Bible as well as in classical literature. *The Odyssey* of Homer describes Ulysses' ten-year journey from Troy to his home in Ithaca, and Bunyan's *Pilgrim's Progress* is an account of Christian's journey from the City of Destruction to the heavenly city. The Bible frequently exhorts us to choose the right path, but the contemporary world thinks there are "many ways to God" and any path you sincerely follow will eventually take you there.

Jesus made it clear that in this life we can take only one of two ways, and each of them leads to a different destination. Everybody has to choose either the crowded road that leads

34

to destruction or the narrow road that leads to life (Matt. 7:13-14). There's no middle way.

In the Book of Proverbs, the words "path" and "way" (and their plurals) are found nearly 100 times (KJV). Wisdom is not only a person to love, but wisdom is also a path to walk, and the emphasis in chapters 2, 3, and 4 is on the blessings God's people enjoy when they walk on Wisdom's path. The path of Wisdom leads to life, but the way of Folly leads to death; when you walk on the path of Wisdom, you enjoy three wonderful assurances: Wisdom *protects* your path (chap. 2), *directs* your path (chap. 3), and *perfects* your path (chap. 4).

1. Wisdom protects your path (Prov. 2)

The key verse in chapter 2 is verse 8: "He guards the paths of justice, and preserves the way of His saints" (NKJV). The repetition of the phrase "my son" (2:1; 3:1, 11, 21; 4:10, 20; and see 4:1, "my children") reminds us that the Book of Proverbs records a loving father's wise counsel to his family. The British statesman Lord Chesterfield said, "In matters of religion and matrimony I never give any advice; because I will not have anybody's torments in this world or the next laid to my charge." But Jewish fathers were *commanded* to teach their children wisdom (Deut. 6:1-9); if the children were smart, they paid attention and obeyed. Life is dangerous. It is wise to listen to the counsel of godly people who have walked the path before us.

Three different "walks" are described in this chapter.

Walking with God (vv. 1-9). Chapters 2–4 all begin with an admonition to listen to God's words and take them to heart (3:1-12; 4:1-9), because that's the only way we can walk with God and live skillfully. Eight imperatives in this paragraph reveal our responsibilities toward God's truth: *receive* (accept) God's words and *hide* them (store them up) in our minds and hearts; *incline* the ear and *apply* the heart; *cry after* knowledge and *lift up the voice* for understanding; *seek* for wisdom and *search after* it. If you want wisdom, you must listen to God attentively (Matt. 13:9), obey Him humbly (John 7:17), ask Him sincerely (James 1:5), and seek Him diligently (Isa. 55:6-7), the way a miner searches for silver and gold.

Obtaining spiritual wisdom isn't a once-a-week hobby, it is the daily discipline of a lifetime. But in this age of microwave ovens, fast foods, digests, and numerous "made easy" books, many people are out of the habit of daily investing time and energy in digging deep into Scripture and learning wisdom from the Lord. Thanks to television, their attention span is brief; thanks to religious entertainment that passes for worship, their spiritual appetite is feeble and spiritual knowledge isn't "pleasant to [their] soul" (Prov. 2:10). It's no wonder fewer and fewer people "take time to be holy" and more and more people fall prey to the enemies that lurk along the way.

If we do our part, God will keep His promise and protect us from the enemy (vv. 7-8): "He holds victory in store for the upright, He is a shield to those whose walk is blameless, for He guards the course of the just and protects the way of His faithful ones" (NIV). "Your word I have hidden in my heart, that I might not sin against You" (Ps. 119:11, NKJV).

People are willing to work diligently in their jobs because they know they'll earn a paycheck, but what about applying themselves diligently to God's Word in order to gain spiritual riches that are more valuable than gold and silver and jewels, riches that will last forever? (See 2:4; 3:13-15; 8:10-21; 16:16.) There's a price to pay if we would gain spiritual wisdom, but there's an even greater price to pay if we don't gain it. We must walk with God through the study of His Word.

Walking with the wicked (vv. 10-19). Here we meet "the evil man" and "the strange woman," two people who are dangerous because they want to lead God's children away from the path of life. The evil man is known for his perverse ("froward," KJV; crooked) words (see vv. 12, 14; 6:14; 8:13; 10:31-32; and 16:28, 30). He walks on the dark path of disobedience and enjoys doing that which is evil. He belongs to the crowd Solomon warns us about in 1:10-19. The person who walks in the way of wisdom would immediately detect his deceit and avoid him.

The "strange woman" is the adulteress, the wayward wife described so vividly in 7:1-27. If the evil man uses *perverse* words to snare the unwary, the adulteress uses *flattering* words. Someone has said that flattery isn't communication, it is manipulation; it's people telling us things about ourselves that we enjoy hearing and wish were true. The strange woman knows how to use flattery successfully. She has no respect for God, because she breaks His law (Ex. 20:14); she has no respect for her husband because she violates the promises she made to him when she married him. She no longer has a guide or a friend in the Lord or in her husband, because she has taken the path of sin. Anyone who listens to her words and follows her path is heading for the cemetery.

Walking with the righteous (vv. 20-22). Note the argument that Solomon gives in this chapter that begins with the "if" of verse 1 and continues with the "then" of verse 9 and the "thus" of verse 20. *If* we receive God's words and obey them, *then* we will have wisdom to make wise decisions, and *thus* God will keep His promise and protect us from the evil man and the strange woman. When you obey God, you have the privilege to "walk in the ways of good men" (v. 20, NIV). *If you follow the Word of God, you will never lack for the right kind of friends.*

The wicked may appear to be succeeding, but their end is destruction (Ps. 37). The godly will be rooted in the place of God's blessing (Ps. 1:3), but the ungodly will be uprooted from the land. The safest and most satisfying path is the path of wisdom, the path of life.

2. Wisdom directs our path (Prov. 3)

The key verses in this chapter are verses 5-6, a promise God's people have often claimed as they have sought the Lord's direction for their lives. And this promise has never failed them — if they have obeyed the conditions God has laid down in verses 1-12. God keeps His promises when we obey His precepts, because our obedience prepares us to receive and enjoy what He has planned for us.

Conditions to meet (vv. 1-12). The first condition for receiving God's guidance is that we *learn God's truth* (vv. 1-4). The will of God is revealed in the Word of God (Col. 1:9-10), and the only way to know His will is to study His Word and obey it. By receiving the Word within our hearts, we experience growth in godly character so that mercy and truth ("love and faithfulness," NIV) become beautiful ornaments in our lives (Prov. 3:3; 1:9). It isn't enough for believers to carry the Bible in their hands; they must let the Holy Spirit write it on their hearts (3:3; 7:3; 2 Cor. 3:1-3). Obedience to the Word can add years to your life and life to your years.

Second, we must *obey God's will* (vv. 5-8). "He shall direct your paths" (v. 6, NKJV) is the promise, but the fulfillment of that promise is predicated on our obedience to the Lord. We must trust Him with all our heart and obey Him in all our ways. That means total commitment to Him (Rom. 12:1-2). The word translated "trust" in verse 5 means "to lie helpless, facedown." It pictures a servant waiting for the master's command in readiness to obey, or a defeated soldier yielding himself to the conquering general.

The danger, of course, is that we lean on our own understanding and thereby miss God's will. This warning doesn't suggest that God's children turn off their brains and ignore their intelligence and common sense. It simply cautions us not to depend on our own wisdom and experience or the wisdom and experience of others. Abraham did this when he went to Egypt (Gen. 12:10-20) and so did Joshua when he attacked the little town of Ai (Josh. 7). When we become "wise in [our] own eyes" (Prov. 3:7), then we're heading for trouble.

Share God's blessings (vv. 9-10) is the third condition we must meet if we want God to direct our paths. There's no such thing as "spiritual" and "material" in the Christian life, for everything comes from God and belongs to God. The Old Testament Jews brought the Lord the firstlings of their flocks (Ex. 13:1-2) and the firstfruits of their fields (Lev. 23:9-14), and in this way acknowledged His goodness and sovereignty. The New Testament parallel is seen in Matthew 6:33.

If we don't faithfully give to the Lord, we don't really trust the Lord. Of course, our tithes and offerings aren't "payment" for His blessings; rather, they're evidence of our faith and obedience. Christian industrialist R.G. LeTourneau used to say, "If you give because it pays, it won't pay." Giving is heart preparation for what God wants to say to us and do for us. "For where your treasure is, there your heart will be also" (Matt. 6:21, NKJV).

Our fourth responsibility is to *submit to God's chastening* (Prov. 3:11-12). Chastening is a part of God's plan to help His sons and daughters mature in godly character (Heb. 12:1-11). God chastens us, not as a judge punishes a criminal, but as a parent disciplines a child. He acts in love and His purpose is that we might become "partakers of His holiness" (Heb. 12:10). Sometimes He chastens because we have rebelled and need to repent; other times He chastens to keep us from sinning and to prepare us for His special blessing. No matter how much the experience *hurts* us, it will never *harm* us, because God always chastens in love (Deut. 8:2-5).

Blessings to enjoy (vv. 13-35). If we trust and obey, our Father will direct our path into the blessings He has planned for us; the first of these blessings is the *true wealth that comes from wisdom* (vv. 13-18). Some people know the price of everything but the value of nothing; consequently, they make unwise choices and end up with shoddy merchandise. An acquaintance of mine, thinking he was getting a bargain, bought a box of white shirts from a street vendor for just a few dollars. When he opened the box at home, he discovered they weren't shirts at all: they were dickeys made to be used on corpses. So much for his bargain. You take what you want from life, and you pay for it.

It's good to have the things money can buy, provided you don't lose the things money can't buy. What good is an expensive house if there's no happy home within it? Happiness, pleasantness, and peace aren't the guaranteed by-products of financial success, but they are guaranteed to the person who lives by God's wisdom. Wisdom becomes a "tree of life" to the believer who takes hold of her, and this is a foretaste of heaven (Rev. 22:1-2).

Another blessing is *harmony with God's creation* (Prov. 3:19-20). The person who walks according to God's wisdom can sing, "This is my Father's world," and really mean it. The wisdom of God brought everything into being (8:22ff), including what science calls "the laws of nature." Obey these laws and creation will work with you; disobey them and creation will work against you. People in the so-called "New Age" movement try to be "at one" with creation, but they're doomed to fail because they reject the wisdom of God. Christians who live by God's wisdom will be good stewards of His creation and will use His gifts for His glory.

A third blessing is *the Father's providential care* (3:21-26). Because God *directs* our path, He is able to *protect* our path. The Lord isn't obligated to protect His children when they willfully go their own way. They're only tempting Him, and that's a dangerous thing to do. Back in the early '40s an angry unbeliever asked a pastor friend of mine, "Why doesn't God stop this terrible war?" My friend quietly replied, "He doesn't stop it because He didn't start it." It was started by people who rejected God's wisdom and pursued their own selfish plans.

When you surrender yourself to God, every part of your body belongs to Him and will be protected by Him. He will help you keep your *eyes* from wandering (v. 21), your *neck* from turning your face away from God's path (vv. 22; see Luke 9:53), your *feet* walking on the right path (Prov. 3:23, 26), and even your *backbone* safe while you're sleeping (v. 24). If something frightening suddenly happens, you won't be afraid (v. 25; see Pss. 112:7; 121:3-6), because the Lord is protecting you. How we sleep is sometimes evidence of how much we trust the Lord (Pss. 4–5).

A *positive relationship with others* (Prov. 3:27-35) is a fourth blessing the believer enjoys when he or she walks in the wisdom of God. Wise Christians will be generous to their neighbors and live peaceably with them (vv. 27-30), doing their best to avoid unnecessary disagreements (Rom. 12:18). After all, if we truly love God, we will love our neighbor as we would want him to love us.

On the other hand, if our neighbor is a perverse person who scoffs at our faith (Prov. 3:31-35), the Lord will guide us in letting our light shine and His love show so that we will influence him but he won't lead us astray. Sometimes it takes a great deal of patience, prayer, and wisdom to rightly relate to people who don't want Christians in the neighborhood, but perhaps that's why God put us there.

It's possible to have a godly home in the midst of an ungodly neighborhood, for God "blesses the home of the righteous" (v. 33, NIV). We are the salt of the earth and the light of the world, and one dedicated Christian in a neighborhood can make a great deal of difference and be a powerful witness for the Lord.

3. Wisdom perfects our path (Prov. 4)

The key verse in chapter 4 is verse 18, "But the path of the just is like the shining light, that shineth more and more unto the perfect day." The picture is that of the sunrise ("the first gleam of dawn," NIV) and the increasing of the light on the pilgrim path as the day advances. If we walk in the way of God's wisdom, the path gets brighter and brighter and there is no sunset! When the path ends, we step into a land where the light never dims, for "there shall be no night there" (Rev. 22:5).

God has a plan for each of His children (Eph. 2:10), and if we walk in His wisdom, we can confidently say, "The Lord will perfect that which concerns me" (Ps. 138:8, NKJV). Our path may not be an easy one, but it will always be a fulfilling one as we walk in the will of the Father. This involves three responsibilities on our part: knowing God's Word (Prov. 4:1-9), trusting God's providence (vv. 10-19), and obeying God's will (vv. 20-27).

Knowing God's Word (vv. 1-9). Some children don't like to hear Dad say, "Now, back when I was a boy . . ." but they might learn a lot if they paid attention and listened. He learned wisdom from his father and now he's passing it on to the next generation. This is the primary way God has ordained for His truth to be preserved and invested from generation to generation (Deut. 6:3-9; Eph. 6:1-4; 2 Tim. 1:3-5; 2:2; 3:14-17). Children who have godly parents and grandparents ought to give thanks to the Lord for their rich heritage, instead of scoffing at that heritage and abandoning it for the way of the world.

"Get wisdom" (Prov. 4:5) suggests, "buy wisdom," because the Hebrew word carries the idea of a commercial transaction. There's a price to pay if you want to know God's truth and obey it. "Buy the truth, and sell it not" (23:23). Parents and grandparents can teach us, but only *we* can re-

ceive the Word into our hearts, cherish it, and pay the price
to obey it.

The father tells his sons to treat wisdom the way they
would treat their mother, sister, or wife: love her, honor her,
embrace her, exalt her! The bumper sticker that asks, "Have
you hugged your children today?" ought to be balanced with,
"Have you hugged wisdom today?" In Proverbs, Wisdom is
personified as a beautiful woman who invites us to her lavish
banquet, while Folly is the adulteress or prostitute who
tempts us to poverty and death. The one you love is the one
who will control your life. Embrace Wisdom and you will have
security (4:6), honor (v. 8), and beauty (v. 9).

Trusting God's providence (vv. 10-19). When you receive
God's truth into your heart, God renews your mind (Rom.
12:2) and enables you to think wisely. This helps you make
right decisions and experience the guidance of God day by
day. God in His loving providence directs us and prepares the
path for us. Augustine said, "Trust the past to the mercy of
God, the present to His love, and the future to His providence." But King David said it better long before Augustine:
"You will show me the path of life; in Your presence is
fullness of joy; at Your right hand are pleasures forevermore"
(Ps. 16:11, NKJV).[1]

If you are willing to do God's will, you will have God's
guidance (John 7:17), but if you treat God's will like a buffet
lunch, choosing only what pleases you, He will never direct
you. As I've said before, the will of God isn't for the curious;
it's for the serious. As we look back on more than forty years
of marriage and ministry, my wife and I can testify to God's
providential leading in our lives in ways that we never sus-
pected He would use.

But God's children can't expect God's leading if they shut-
tle back and forth between the path of wisdom and the path of
the wicked (Prov. 4:14-17). Stay as far away from that path as

you can! Don't enter it! Avoid it! Don't go near it! Go as far from it as you can! Certainly we must witness to unsaved people whom the Lord brings to us, but we must never adopt their lifestyle or imitate their ways. *God doesn't guide His children when they're walking in darkness.* When you're living in the will of God, the path gets brighter and brighter, not darker and darker (1 John 1:5-10).

The danger is that we let the lessons of wisdom slip through our fingers and we lose them. "Take fast hold of instruction; let her not go" (Prov. 4:13). Hold on to wisdom the way a child holds a parent's hand and trusts Mother or Father to guide and protect. God is able to keep us from stumbling (Jude 24) if we'll keep ourselves in His wisdom.

Obeying God's will (vv. 20-27). This is a wonderful paragraph to us as a personal spiritual inventory to see if we're really living in obedience to the Lord. Let's ask ourselves:

"What comes into my ears?" (v. 20) Whatever enters my ears will ultimately influence my mind, my heart, and my decisions, so I'd better be careful what I listen to. Paul warns us to beware of "obscenity, foolish talk or coarse joking" (Eph. 5:4, NIV), and Psalm 1:1 tells us to avoid ungodly counsel. When people speak, we must be able to identify God's voice (John 10:3-5, 16) and obey what He says.

"What is within my heart?" (v. 23) Whatever the heart loves, the ears will hear and the eyes will see. When our children were small, no matter where we were driving, they could usually find the ice cream shops and the toy stores; I must confess that I managed to locate the bookstores! "Above all else, guard your heart, for it is the wellspring of life" (v. 23, NIV). If we pollute that wellspring, the infection will spread; before long, hidden appetites will become open sins and public shame.

The Bible warns us to avoid a double heart (Ps. 12:2), a hard heart (Prov. 28:14), a proud heart (21:4), an unbelieving heart (Heb. 3:12), a cold heart (Matt. 24:12), and an unclean heart (Ps. 51:10). "Search me, O God, and know my heart" (139:23).

"What is upon my lips?" (v. 24) Whatever is in the heart will ultimately come out of the mouth (Matt. 12:33-34). God's children must be careful to have "sound speech that cannot be condemned" (Titus 2:8), speech that's gracious and "seasoned with salt" (Col. 4:6, NKJV). The ancient Romans, listening to one of their orators, would look at each other, smile, and say, "Cum grano salis" — "Take it with a grain of salt." But Christians are supposed to *put the salt into their speech* and keep their words pure and honest.

As we shall see in a later chapter, Proverbs has a great deal to say about human speech; in fact, the word "mouth" is used over fifty times and the word "lips" over forty times in the *Authorized Version.* Among other things, Solomon warns us about perverse lips (Prov. 4:24), lying lips (12:22), flattering lips (20:19), deceptive lips (24:28), and undisciplined lips (10:19). "He who guards his lips guards his life, but he who speaks rashly will come to ruin" (13:3, NIV).

"What is before my eyes?" (v. 25) Outlook determines outcome. Abraham was the friend of God because he walked by faith and "looked for a city . . . whose builder and maker is God" (Heb. 11:10). Lot became a friend of the world because he walked by sight and moved toward the wicked city of Sodom (Gen. 13:10, 12). Everybody has some vision before them that helps to determine their values, actions, and plans. We would all be wise to imitate David who said, "I will set no wicked thing before mine eyes" (Ps. 101:3), and the writer of Psalm 119 who prayed, "Turn my eyes away from worthless things" (v. 37, NIV). If you are "looking unto Jesus" (Heb. 12:2) as you walk the path of life, then keep that posture of faith. If you look back (Luke 9:62) or around (Matt. 14:30), you may go on a detour.

"What is beyond my path?" *(vv. 26-27)* The Hebrew word translated "ponder" means "to weigh" or "to make level." It is related to a word that means "scales" (16:11). In his final speech before he drank the hemlock, Socrates said, "The unexamined life is not worth living"; Paul wrote, "Examine yourselves as to whether you are in the faith. Test yourselves" (2 Cor. 13:5, NKJV). The Lord is weighing our ways (Prov. 5:21) and our hearts (21:2), as well as our actions (1 Sam. 2:3), and we had better do the same. Life is too short and too precious to be wasted on the temporary and the trivial.

If we're walking in the way of wisdom, God promises to protect our path, direct our path, and perfect our path.

All folly can offer us is danger, detours, and disappointments, ultimately leading to death.

It shouldn't be too difficult to make the right choice!

FOUR

The Path of Folly and Death

Y ou shall not commit adultery."
The Lord God spoke those words at Mount Sinai, and we call what He said the Seventh Commandment (Ex. 20:14). It declares that sexual intimacy outside the bonds of marriage is wrong, even if "between consenting adults."[1] This law specifically mentions adultery, but the commandment includes the sexual sins prohibited elsewhere in Scripture (Lev. 18; Rom. 1:18-32; 1 Cor. 6:9-20; Eph. 5:1-14). God invented sex and has every right to tell us how to use it properly.

However, on hearing the Seventh Commandment, many people in contemporary society smile nonchalantly and ask, "What's wrong with premarital or extramarital sex, or any other kind, for that matter?" After all, they argue, many people indulge in these things and seem to get away with it. Furthermore, these activities are more acceptable today than they were in Solomon's day; why make a big issue out of it? "Life is a game in which the rules are constantly changing," says a contemporary writer; "nothing spoils a game more than those who take it seriously."[2] So, the verdict's in: sex is fun, so don't take it too seriously.

It's true that some well-known people have indulged in sexual escapades and even bragged about it, including government officials, Hollywood stars, sports heroes, and (alas!) preachers, but that doesn't make it right. Sexual sin is one of the main themes of numerous movies, TV programs, novels, and short stories; yet popularity is no test of right and wrong. Many things that the law says are legal, the Bible says are evil, and there won't be a jury sitting at the White Throne Judgment (Rev. 20:11-15; 21:27; 22:15).

Why worry about sexual sins? These three chapters of Proverbs give us three reasons why we should worry if we break God's laws of purity: because sexual sin is eventually disappointing (Prov. 5), gradually destructive (chap. 6), and ultimately deadly (chap. 7). That's why God says, "You shall not commit adultery."

1. Sexual sin is eventually disappointing (Prov. 5)

When married people honor and respect sex as God instructs them in His Word, they can experience increasing enjoyment and enrichment in their intimacy. But when people break the rules, the result is just the opposite. They experience disappointment and disillusionment and have to search for larger "doses" of sexual adventure in order to attain the imaginary pleasure level they're seeking.

God created sex not only for reproduction but also for enjoyment, and He didn't put the "marriage wall" around sex to *rob* us of pleasure but to *increase* pleasure and *protect* it. In this chapter, Solomon explains the disappointments that come when people violate God's loving laws of sexual purity.

Their experience goes from sweetness to bitterness (vv. 1-6). We've met "the strange woman" before (2:16; NIV, "adulteress") and she'll be mentioned again (5:20; 6:24; 7:5; 20:16; 22:14; 23:27; 27:13). The word translated "strange" basically means "not related to." The "strange woman" is one to whom the man is not related by marriage, and therefore any sexual liaison with her is evil. The beginning of this sinful alliance may be exciting and sweet, because the kisses and words from her lips drip like honey (7:13-20), but in the end, the "sweetness" turns to bitterness and the honey becomes poison (5:4).

The Book of Proverbs emphasizes the importance of *looking ahead to see where your actions will lead you* (see 5:11; 14:12-14; 16:25; 19:20; 20:21; 23:17-18, 32; 24:14, 20; 25:8). The wise person checks on the destination before buying a ticket (4:26), but modern society thinks that people can violate God's laws and escape the consequences. They're sure that whatever has happened to others will never happen to them. Sad to say, their ignorance and insolence can never neutralize the tragic aftermath that comes when people break the laws of God. "Oh, that they were wise, that they understood this, that they would consider their latter end!" (Deut. 32:29)

Their experience goes from gain to loss (vv. 7-14). Temptation always includes hopeful promises; otherwise, people would never take the devil's bait. For a time, it seems like these promises have been fulfilled, and sinners bask in the sunshine of pleasant experiences and false assurances. This is what family counselor J. Allan Petersen calls, "the myth of the greener grass."[3] People who commit sexual sins think their problems are solved ("She understands me so much better than my wife does!") and that life will get better and better. But disobedience to God's laws always brings sad consequences and sinners eventually pay dearly for their brief moments of pleasure.

When you read verses 9-14, you hear the words of a suffering sinner lamenting the high cost of disobeying God's laws, because *the most expensive thing in the world is sin.* He discovers that the woman's husband is a cruel man who demands that he pay for what he's done, so the adulterer ends up giving his strength to others and toiling away to pay his debt. Instead of luxury, the sinner has misery; instead of riches, poverty; instead of success, ruin; and instead of a good reputation, the name of an adulterer. He looks back and wishes he had listened to his parents and his spiritual instructors, but his wishes can't change his wretched situation. Yes, God in His *grace* will forgive his sins if he repents, but God in His *government* sees to it that he reaps what he sows.

Their experience goes from purity to pollution (vv. 15-20). Solomon compares enjoying married love to drinking pure water from a fresh well, but committing sexual sin is like drinking polluted water from the gutter or sewer. Sex within marriage is a beautiful river that brings life and refreshment, but sex outside marriage is a sewer that defiles everything it touches. To commit sexual sin is to pour this beautiful river into the streets and the public squares. What waste! If you "drink deep" of the wrong kind of love (7:18, NIV) it will destroy you.

The commitment of marriage is like the banks of the river that keep the river from becoming a swamp. God's holy law confines the waters within the banks, and this produces power and depth. Extramarital and premarital affairs don't satisfy because they're shallow, and it doesn't take much to stir up shallow water. A man and woman pledged to each other in marriage can experience the growing satisfaction that comes with love, commitment, depth, and purity.

But there's something else involved here. Solomon admonishes the husband to be "ravished" with his wife's love (5:19-20); the word translated "ravished" also means "intoxicated" or "infatuated."[4] The adulterer watches the river turn into a sewer, but the faithful husband sees the water become wine! I think it's significant that Jesus turned water into wine at a wedding feast, as though He were giving us an object lesson concerning the growing delights of marriage (John 2:1-11).

When a husband and wife are faithful to the Lord and to each other, and when they obey Scriptures like 1 Corinthians 7:1-5 and Ephesians 5:22-33, neither of them will look for satisfaction anywhere else. If they love each other and seek to please each other and the Lord, their relationship will be one of deepening joy and satisfaction; they won't look around for "the greener grass."

Their experience goes from freedom to bondage (vv. 21-23). Freedom of choice is one of the privileges God has given us, but He instructs us and urges us to use that freedom wisely. The laws of God are guideposts to lead us on the path of life, and He watches the decisions we make and the roads we take. "The eyes of the Lord are in every place, beholding the evil and the good" (15:3).

As long as we use our freedom wisely, we will mature in Christian character, and God can trust us with more freedom. But if we abuse our freedom and deliberately disobey His Word, our freedom will gradually become bondage, the kind of bondage that can't easily be broken. "The evil deeds of a wicked man ensnare him; the cords of his sin hold him fast" (5:22, NIV). Those words could have been used as an epitaph for Samson (Jud. 13–16).

It's impossible to sin without being bound. One of the deceitful things about sin is that it promises freedom but only brings slavery. "Most assuredly, I say to you, whoever commits sin is a slave of sin" (John 8:34, NKJV). "Do you not know that to whom you present yourselves slaves to obey, you are that one's slaves whom you obey, whether of sin leading to death, or of obedience leading to righteousness?" (Rom. 6:16, NKJV)

The cords of sin get stronger the more we sin, yet sin deceives us into thinking we're free and can quit sinning whenever we please. As the invisible chains of habit are forged, we discover to our horror that we don't have the strength to break them. Millions of people in our world today are in one kind of bondage or another and are seeking for deliverance, but the only One who can set them free is Jesus Christ. "Therefore if the Son makes you free, you shall be free indeed" (John 8:36, NKJV).

No wonder the father warns his children to stay away from the adulteress. "Remove your way far from her, and do not go near the door of her house" (Prov. 5:8, NKJV). "Her house is the way to hell, going down to the chambers of death" (7:27).

2. Sexual sin is gradually destructive (Prov. 6)

Chapter 6 deals with three enemies that can destroy a person financially, physically, morally, or spiritually: unwise financial commitments (vv. 1-5), laziness (vv. 6-11), and lust (vv. 20-35). It is not unusual for one person to be guilty of all three, because laziness and lust often go together; people who can easily be pressured into putting up security for somebody can be pressured into doing other foolish things, including committing adultery. "For where your treasure is, there will your heart be also" (Matt. 6:21).

We will consider Proverbs 6:1-11 in our study of wealth and work. Verses 12-19 will be included in chapter 5, in our study of "the wicked people" mentioned in the Book of Proverbs. In verses 20-35, Solomon deals with adultery and points out what people will lose who commit this heinous sin.

They lose the Word of God (vv. 20-24). In chapters 5–7, each of the warnings against adultery is prefaced by an admonition to pay attention to the Word of God (5:1-2; 6:20-24; 7:1-5). It is by our trusting and obeying His truth that God keeps us from believing the enemy's lies. Certainly children have the obligation to honor their father and mother (6:20; see 1:8), and God's children have the responsibility and privilege of bringing glory to their Father's name. "Marriage is honorable among all, and the bed undefiled; but fornicators and adulterers God will judge" (Heb. 13:4, NKJV).

The Word should be bound to the heart (Ps. 119:11), because the heart is "the wellspring of life" (Prov. 4:23, NIV).[5] God's truth should also control the neck, because a man might be tempted to turn his head and look at a beautiful woman for the purpose of lusting (Matt. 5:27-30). He may not be able to avoid seeing the woman the first time, but it's looking the second time that gets him into trouble.

The Word of God in the mind and heart is like a guide who leads us on the safe path and protects us from attacks. It's also like a friend who talks to us and counsels us along the way (Prov. 6:22). We walk in the light because the Word is a lamp (v. 23; Ps. 119:105, 130). If we listen to God's voice in His Word, we won't fall for the enemy's flattery (Prov. 6:24).

Read 1 John 1:5-10 and note that "walking in the light" assures us of hearing the Word of God, while "walking in darkness" causes us to lose His Word. If we disobey Him, we don't *do* the truth (Prov. 6:6), we don't *have* the truth (v. 8), and *His Word is not in us* (v. 10). There is a gradual erosion of the spiritual life, from light to darkness, and with this erosion comes a deterioration of Christian character.

They lose wealth (vv. 25-26). This parallels 5:7-14, and see 29:3. To be "brought to a piece of bread" means to be degraded to the lowest level of poverty (see Luke 15:13-16, 30). If the adultery results in scandal, a lawsuit, and a divorce, the price will not be cheap; in this day of AIDS and other sexually transmitted diseases, the adulterer is taking chances with his health and his life.

They lose enjoyment (vv. 27-31). Fire is a good thing if it's confined and controlled. It can keep us warm, cook our food, drive our turbines, and manufacture our electricity. Sex is a good gift from God but, like fire, if it gets out of control, it becomes destructive. What begins as a "warm" experience soon becomes a burning experience, like holding a torch in your lap or walking on burning coals.

"But sex is a normal desire, given to us by God," some people argue. "Therefore, we have every right to use it, even if we're not married. It's like eating: If you're hungry, God gave you food to eat; if you're lonely, God gave you sex to enjoy." Some of the people in the Corinthian church used this argument to defend their sinful ways: "Foods for the stomach and the stomach for foods" (1 Cor. 6:13, NKJV). But Paul made it clear that the believer's body belonged to God and that the presence of a desire wasn't the same as the privilege to satisfy that desire (vv. 12-20).

Solomon used a similar approach in Proverbs 6:30-31. Certainly hunger is a strong force in human life, and the only way to satisfy hunger is to eat, but if you steal the bread that you eat, you're breaking the law. You'll end up paying more for that bread than if you'd gone out and bought a loaf at the bakery. As you sit in jail or stand in court, the enjoyment you had from that bread will soon be forgotten.

Adultery is stealing. "For this is the will of God, your sanctification; that is, that you abstain from sexual immorality . . . and that no man transgress and defraud his brother in the matter" (1 Thes. 4:3, 6, NASB). When adultery enters a marriage, everybody loses.

They lose their good sense (v. 32). King David was a brilliant strategist on the battlefield and a wise ruler on the throne, but he lost his common sense when he gazed at his neighbor's wife and lusted for her (2 Sam. 12). He was sure he could get away with his sin, but common sense would have told him he was wrong. Every stratagem David used to implicate Bathsheba's husband failed, so he ended up having the man killed. Surely David knew that we reap what we sow, and reap he did, right in the harvest field of his own family.

They lose their peace (vv. 33-35). The angry husband will use every means possible to avenge himself, for a loving husband would rather that his neighbor steal his money than steal his wife. "For love is as strong as death, its jealousy unyielding as the grave. It burns like blazing fire, like a mighty flame" (Song 8:6, NIV). The offender will have no peace, and no amount of money he offers the husband will be accepted. The adulterer loses his reputation in the community and might actually suffer physical punishment. Of course, he and the woman were supposed to be stoned to death (Lev. 20:10; Deut. 22:22), but we're not sure this penalty was always exacted.

In today's society, if a person has enough money and "clout," he or she might be able to survive an adulterous scandal, but life is still never quite the same. Whether in this life or the next, sinners can be sure that their sins will find them out. Indulging in sexual sin is always a losing proposition.

3. Sexual sin is ultimately deadly (Prov. 7)

For the third time, Solomon calls the young person back to the Word of God (vv. 1-5), because keeping God's commandments is a matter of life or death. The adulteress lives on a dead-end street: "Her house is the way to hell, going down to the chambers of death" (v. 27).

The familiar phrase "apple of your eye" (v. 2) refers to the pupil of the eye which the ancients thought was a sphere like an apple. We protect our eyes because they're valuable to us, and so should we honor and protect God's Word by obeying it. Sexual sin often begins with undisciplined eyes and hands (Matt. 5:27-30), but the heart of the problem is . . . the heart (Prov. 7:2-3). If we love God's wisdom as we love those in our family, we wouldn't want to visit the house of the harlot.

This chapter vividly describes a naive young man who falls

into the trap of the adulteress. Note the steps that lead to his destruction.

He tempts himself (vv. 6-9). You get the impression that this young man is either terribly dumb or very proud, convinced that he can play with sin and get away with it. But he's only tempting himself and heading for trouble. To begin with, he's out at night ("walking in darkness"—see 2:13; John 3:19-21; 1 John 1:5-7), and he's deliberately walking near the place of temptation and danger. He didn't heed the wise counsel of the Lord, "Remove your way far from her, and do not go near the door of her house" (5:8, NKJV). God's Word wasn't controlling his feet (3:26; 4:27).

During more than forty years of ministry, I've listened to many sad stories from people who have indulged in sexual sin and suffered greatly; in almost every instance, the people deliberately put themselves into the place of temptation and danger. Unlike Job, they didn't make "a covenant with [their] eyes not to look lustfully at a girl" (Job 31:1, NIV), nor did they follow the example of Joseph and flee from temptation (Gen. 39:7ff; 2 Tim. 2:22). We can't help being tempted, but we can certainly help tempting ourselves.

He is tempted by the woman (vv. 10-20). Like the deadly spider in the web, the woman was watching at the window, ready to pounce on her prey. She was a man's wife, but when he was out of town, she dressed like a prostitute so she could attract the men who were searching for her services (Gen. 38:14-15; Ezek. 16:16). While her husband was away, she saw no reason why she shouldn't make some money and enjoy herself at the same time. She'd been in the streets, looking for victims (Prov. 7:11-12), but now one was coming right to her door!

She caught him (Gen. 39:12), kissed him (Prov. 5:3), and convinced him that it was an opportune time for him to visit her. Before leaving town, her husband had gone with her to the temple where he'd sacrificed a peace offering (Lev. 7:11-21), and she had some of the meat at home. She would prepare him a feast that he would never forget. "This is the way of an adulterous woman: She eats and wipes her mouth, and says, 'I have done no wickedness' " (Prov. 30:20, NKJV).

She appeals to the young man's male ego as she flatters him and makes him think he's very special to her. What she's offering to him she would never offer to anyone else! She appeals to his imagination as she describes her beautiful bed and the expensive spices that perfume it. She assures him that nobody will find out about it (except that somebody's watching, 7:6) and that her husband won't be home for many days. They have plenty of time to enjoy themselves.

He tempts the Lord (vv. 21-27). When we pray, "Lead us not into temptation" (Matt. 6:13), we know that God doesn't tempt us (James 1:13-16); yet we may tempt ourselves, tempt others, and even tempt God (Ex. 17:1-7; Num. 14:22; Deut. 6:16; Ps. 78:18, 56; 1 Cor. 10:9). We tempt God when we deliberately disobey Him and put ourselves into situations so difficult that only God can deliver us. It's as though we "dare Him" to do something.

The youth made a sudden decision to follow the woman, and when he did, he began to act like an animal. He was no longer a young man, made in the image of God, but an ox going to the slaughter or a bird walking into the trap. Human beings are the only creatures in God's creation who can choose what kind of creatures they want to be. God wants us to be sheep (Ps. 23:1; John 10; 1 Peter 2:25), but there are other options, such as horses or mules (Ps. 32:9), or even hogs and dogs (2 Peter 2:22). When we live outside the will of God, we lose our privileges as human beings made in His divine image.

By going to her house, her table, and her bed, the young man willfully disobeyed God's Law, *but the Lord didn't inter-*

vene. He allowed the youth to indulge in his sensual appetites and suffer the consequences. God could have stopped him, but He didn't, because the Word says, "You shall not tempt [put to the test] the Lord your God" (Matt. 4:7; Deut. 6:16). If instead of tempting the Lord, the youth had *looked up* to the Lord and remembered His Word (Prov. 7:24), *looked within* and kept his heart focused on God's truth (v. 25), and *looked ahead* to see the terrible consequences of his sin (vv. 26-27), he would have turned around and fled from the harlot's clutches.

Society today not only smiles at sexual sin, it actually approves it and encourages it. Perversions the very mention of which would have shocked people fifty years ago are openly discussed today and are even made the subject of novels, movies, and TV dramas. What Paul saw in his day and described in Romans 1:18-32 is now apparent in our own day, but people resent it if you call these practices "sin." After all, "Everybody's doing it."

But the Gospel is still "the power of God unto salvation" (Rom. 1:16) and Christ can still change people's lives (1 Cor. 6:9-11). It isn't enough for Christians to protest the evil; we must also practice the good (Matt. 5:13-16) and proclaim the good news that sinners can become new creatures in Christ (2 Cor. 5:17).

If the world had more light, there would be less darkness.

If the world had more salt, there would be less decay.

If the world heard more truth, there would be less deception.

We have a job to do!

INTERLUDE

From this chapter on, we'll be studying the Book of Proverbs *topically,* bringing together texts that deal with the same subjects and showing how they relate to each other and to your personal Christian life today. In a sense, we'll be studying what the Bible teaches about practical Christian living, using the Book of Proverbs as our point of reference.

No classification of texts is inspired or final, and many verses could be put into several different categories. The psalmist was right when he said, "To all perfection I see a limit, but Your commands are boundless" (Ps. 119:96, NIV). Since I won't be quoting every relevant verse, be sure to look up and read the references that I give. It's important that you ponder these Scriptures if you want to get the full benefit of your study.

The easiest way to *study* Proverbs is by topics, but the best way to *read* Proverbs is chapter by chapter, just the way it's written. Why? Because each chapter presents a variety of truths, and you never know which one you will need for any given day. In fact, some verses are repeated so that we'll be sure to get the message.

"The fear of the Lord is the beginning of knowledge" (Prov. 1:7), so keep your heart reverent before Him, and be willing to obey what He says to you.

FIVE

People, Wise and Otherwise — Part 1 (The Wise and the Wicked)

If you carefully watch the crowds in a shopping mall, you'll discover that there are all kinds of people in this world; no doubt the crowds are coming to the same conclusion as they look at you. Playwright George Bernard Shaw said, "If the other planets are inhabited, they're using the earth for their insane asylum." No wonder Charles M. Schulz has his comic strip character Linus exclaim, "I love mankind. It's people I can't stand!"

The Book of Proverbs is basically about different kinds of people, what they believe and do, and how they interact with one another. People create circumstances that are good and bad, and you and I have to deal with people and circumstances as we go through life. Solomon's aim in writing this book is to help us become skillful in relating to both people and circumstances so that we can make a success out of life to the glory of God.

During our survey of Proverbs 1–9, we casually met five different kinds of people: the wise, the wicked, the fool, the simple, and the scorner. Now it's time to get better acquainted with these people and learn what it really means to be wise.

1. The wise

The entire Book of Proverbs is a guide to attaining wisdom, but here and there Solomon points out several important characteristics of the wise man and woman. Of course, the first step toward wisdom is *saving faith in Jesus Christ.* Wise people are "wise unto salvation" (2 Tim. 3:15) before they gain wisdom about anything else, because Jesus Christ is the Wisdom of God (Col. 2:3; 1 Cor. 1:30). Educated and trained people who ignore or reject Christ can succeed in making a good *living,* but without Him they can never succeed in making a good *life* — one that glorifies God. The wisest thing a person can do is to trust Christ and live in obedience to Him.

Let's consider some of the important characteristics of wise people.

Wise people listen to wise instruction, especially the Word of God. "A wise man[1] will hear, and will increase learning" (1:5). Wise people pay attention to spoken instruction as well as to the written Word of God (22:17-21). Jesus warns us to take heed *what* we hear (Mark 4:24) and *how* we hear (Luke 8:18). "Stop listening to instruction, my son, and you will stray from the words of knowledge" (Prov. 19:27, NIV). "Buy the truth, and do not sell it, also wisdom and instruction and understanding" (23:23, NKJV). It costs to acquire wisdom, but it's worth it!

This means that we must diligently spend time reading and studying the Word of God, appropriating its truths into our hearts, and obeying what God commands (2:1-9). It isn't enough to own a study Bible and read books about the Bible, helpful as they are. It's one thing to know about the Bible and quite something else to hear God speak through His Word and teach us His wisdom so that we become more like Jesus Christ. During my many years of ministry, I've met a few people whose knowledge of Scripture was phenomenal, but who failed to manifest the fruit of the Spirit (Gal. 5:22-23).

"Knowledge puffs up, but love builds up" (1 Cor. 8:1, NIV).

But there's a negative side to this as well: Wise people don't waste their time listening to foolishness and lies. Wise people are careful about what they read, what they hear and see, and what they talk about in daily conversation. They're diligent to keep trash out of their minds and hearts, because "garbage in" ultimately means "garbage out" (see Prov. 4:23). For this reason, they carefully control the radio and television and they are selective in their reading.

Those who are wise profit from rebuke (9:8-9; 10:17; 17:10) and from advice (13:10; 12:15; 19:20). They don't think so highly of themselves that they can't learn from others (3:7; 26:12). If we're "wise in our own eyes," we certainly won't be wise in God's eyes!

Wise people fear the Lord. "The fear of the Lord is the beginning of wisdom" (1:7). "Do not be wise in your own eyes; fear the Lord and depart from evil" (3:7). We've already learned that "fearing the Lord" means respecting Him so that we obey His will and seek to honor His name. Fearing the Lord is the opposite of tempting the Lord by deliberately disobeying Him and then daring Him to intervene. "Work out your own salvation with fear and trembling" (Phil. 2:12). "Serve the Lord with fear, and rejoice with trembling" (Ps. 2:11).

The fear of the Lord is "a fountain of life" (Prov. 14:27) and leads to life (19:23). It gives security (14:26), hope (23:17-18), and the promise of long life (10:27). When you fear the Lord, you keep your priorities straight. "Better is a little with the fear of the Lord, than great treasure with trouble" (15:16, NKJV). You also steer clear of evil (8:13; 16:6; see also 14:2).

Wise people associate with wise people. "He who walks with wise men will be wise, but the companion of fools will be destroyed" (13:20, NKJV). As we read and study Scripture, we associate with the wise men and women of Bible history and learn from them. By spending time with godly friends, we can learn wisdom and grow in our knowledge of Christ. As I look back over my Christian pilgrimage, I thank God for the many people the Lord brought into my life to help me better understand the wisdom and ways of the Lord. "A righteous man is cautious in friendship, but the way of the wicked leads them astray" (12:26, NIV).

One of the best ways to "walk with the wise" is to read church history and Christian biography. I have hundreds of volumes of biography and autobiography in my library, some of which I have read many times, and these books have greatly enriched my life. I didn't have the privilege of knowing personally J. Hudson Taylor, Amy Carmichael, St. Augustine, Dwight L. Moody, Billy Sunday, G. Campbell Morgan, Fanny Crosby, or Robert Murray M'Cheyne, but by reading their biographies and autobiographies, sermons and letters, I've benefited from their walk with the Lord.

Wise people preserve what they've gained and they use it. "Wise people store up knowledge, but the mouth of the foolish is near destruction" (10:14, NKJV). If wisdom is stored in the heart, then we'll say the right thing at the right time, and people will be helped. But fools lose whatever wisdom they may have picked up, and their words only bring destruction.

A parallel text is 12:27: "The lazy man does not roast his game, but the diligent man prizes his possessions" (NIV). The Scottish preacher George Morrison has a powerful sermon on this text entitled "Wasted Gains."[2] (The very title is a sermon!) What a tragedy it is when people waste their gains by failing to use their education, the sermons and Bible lessons they've heard, or the books they've read. Truly wise people treasure the knowledge and skills they've worked hard to acquire and use this treasure to the glory of God.

I recall hearing some of my student friends say at seminary graduation, "Thank the Lord, no more Greek and Hebrew!"

They had spent several years learning to use the Bible languages, and now they were selling their valuable language tools and thereby wasting their gains.

Over the years, I have made good use of wide-margin Bibles in which I've written the things God's taught me and that I've learned from others. Many times while preparing a sermon or writing a book, I have turned to these notes and "invested" my gains. When I read a good book, I underline important sentences, write notes in the margins, and compile my own index of ideas at the back of the book. My copier gets plenty of use because I copy material from books and put it into file folders for future use. This way I'm not wasting my gains.

Wise people flee from sin. "A wise man fears and departs from evil, but a fool rages and is self-confident" (14:16, NKJV). If we fear the Lord, we will hate evil (8:13; see Ps. 97:10; Rom. 12:9). The self-confident person isn't wise. Joshua was self-confident and lost a battle (Josh. 7); Samson was self-confident and became a prisoner (Jud. 16:20ff); Peter was self-confident and betrayed the Lord three times (Luke 22:33-34). "Therefore let him who thinks he stands take heed lest he fall" (1 Cor. 10:12, NKJV).

Wise people don't take unnecessary chances and experiment to see how close they can get to the precipice without falling off. When Joseph was confronted with evil, he fled (Gen. 39:7ff). I heard about a handsome assistant pastor who was being pursued by several young ladies in the church, and the senior minister warned him to be careful.

"Oh, there's safety in numbers," the young man replied rather flippantly, defending himself. To which the senior minister wisely replied, "Yes, there's safety in numbers; but sometimes there's more safety in exodus." Paul would have agreed with the older pastor, for he wrote to Timothy, "Flee youthful lusts" (2 Tim. 2:22).

Wise people discipline their speech. "A wise man's heart guides his mouth, and his lips promote instruction" (Prov. 16:23, NIV). "In the multitude of words sin is not lacking, but he who restrains his lips is wise" (10:19, NKJV). Proverbs has so much to say about the dynamics and dangers of human speech that we'll devote an entire chapter to this topic. Suffice it to say now that the wise person realizes the power of the tongue and keeps it under God's control. "The fruit of the Spirit is . . . self-control" (Gal. 5:22-23; see James 3). The speech of wise people will instruct and inspire, and you're nourished as you listen; the talk of fools only tears down and leaves you empty and discouraged (note Eph. 5:1-7).

Wise people are diligent in their work. "Lazy hands make a man poor, but diligent hands bring wealth. He who gathers crops in summer is a wise son, but he who sleeps during harvest is a disgraceful son" (Prov. 10:4, NIV). Diligence and laziness are key topics in Proverbs, and we'll study them later in greater detail. Solomon makes it clear that God has nothing good to say about careless, lazy people. Wise people are working people, people who make the most of their opportunities and who carry their share of the load. My friend Dr. Bob Cook used to say that hard work is a thrill and a joy when you're doing the will of God; Scottish novelist George MacDonald said, "It's our best work that He wants, not the dregs of our exhaustion."

Wise people seek to influence others to trust the Lord. "The fruit of the righteous is a tree of life, and he who wins souls is wise" (11:30, NKJV). The word translated "wins" means "to capture," as a hunter captures his prey. Wise people seek to capture the ignorant and disobedient by sharing God's wisdom with them. Jesus told His fishermen disciples that they would be "catching men" instead of catching fish (Luke 5:10). Wisdom leads to righteousness, and righteousness produces fruit ("a tree of life"), and this fruit "entices" those who are hungry for what is real and eternal. By both their lives and their words, wise people seek to lead others to the Lord.

As we continue our study of Proverbs, we'll discover other personal characteristics of those who are wise; I trust we'll seek to imitate them. After all, God promises that the wise will inherit glory (3:35), bring joy to others (10:1; 15:20), bring help from God (12:18), never be in want (21:10), and have strength to wage war (24:5-6). The way of wisdom is the way of true life.

2. The wicked

The wicked and their wickedness are mentioned at least 100 times in Proverbs, usually in contrast to the good and the righteous. Proverbs 6:12-19 is somewhat of a summary statement that describes the evil person and the hateful[3] sins that he commits.

The wicked are "naughty," that is, worth nothing (naught), without profit. It's the Hebrew word *belial* (*beli*, without; *ya-al*, profit), used to describe worthless people (Deut. 13:13; Jud. 19:22; 1 Sam. 25:25; 1 Kings 21:10, 13). Sin is not only destructive, it's also unproductive.

Every part of the wicked person's anatomy is devoted to evil and his "body language" communicates evil (see Rom. 3:10-18). His mouth is perverse (froward, KJV), a word that means "crooked, twisted." He can't be trusted. When he wants to signal his confederates that it's time to do evil, he winks his eye, shuffles his feet, and motions with his fingers; they get the message. The cause of all this evil is the perversity of his inner person, for it is out of the heart that evil comes (Mark 7:14-23; Jer. 17:9). He's skillful at plotting evil and the result is dissension. He's a troublemaker who sows discord, but judgment is certain and will come when he least expects it. How much better it is when the whole body is yielded to God (Rom. 12:1-2) and controlled by His Word! (Prov. 4:20-27)

You see these sinful characteristics manifested in the specific sins described in Proverbs 6:16-19, sins that God hates.

First on the list is *pride,* because pride is usually the basic motivation for all other sins. It was pride that turned Lucifer into Satan (Isa. 14:12-14) and that led Eve to disobey God and eat the forbidden fruit (Gen. 3:1-6; note "you shall be as God"). "The fear of the Lord is to hate evil; pride and arrogance and the evil way and the perverse mouth I hate" (Prov. 8:13).

God also hates a *lying tongue,* for God is a God of truth (Deut. 32:4; John 14:6; 1 John 5:6), and His Law says, "Thou shalt not bear false witness" (Ex. 20:16). God sees a lie, not as an act of speech but as a deadly force that goes to work in society and divides and destroys. When we lie, we open the door for Satan to work, for he is a liar (John 8:44); when we speak truth, we give opportunity for the Spirit to work (Eph. 4:14-25). There is a place reserved in hell for liars (Rev. 21:8, 27; see 2 Thes. 2:10).

The third sin God hates is *murder,* "hands that shed innocent blood." His commandment is, "Thou shalt not kill [murder]" (Ex. 20:13). God permits the government to exercise capital punishment and strengthen justice in the land (Gen. 9:5-6; Rom. 13:1-7), but the shedding of innocent blood pollutes the land (Num. 35:30-34). Murderers have their part in the lake of fire (Rev. 21:8; 22:15).

A heart that devises wicked schemes (NIV) is hateful to God because it's a misuse of the great gift of imagination that He has given us. (See Gen. 6:5; 8:21; Jer. 23:17; Rom. 1:21.) The imagination is the "womb" out of which either evil or good is born. People who can plan evil things that hurt others can also plan good things that will help others. The imagination needs to be cleansed and kept pure before God so He can use it in His service. Only God can change the sinful heart (Jer. 31:33-34; Heb. 10:14-18; Ps. 51:10), and God's people must take care to guard their hearts against evil (Prov. 4:23).

Sinners have *feet that are swift in running to mischief [evil]* because they want to fulfill their schemes quickly and enjoy their pleasures immediately. God's people should have cleansed feet (John 13:1-17; 1 John 1:9), beautiful feet (Rom. 10:14-15), prepared feet (Eph. 6:15), and obedient feet (Gen. 13:17; Josh. 1:3; 3:15). If we do, we'll bring blessing. But the wicked use their feet to get involved in sin: meddling as busybodies (2 Thes. 3:11; 1 Tim. 5:13), tempting others into sin (Prov. 5:5 and 7:11), and breaking God's laws (1:10-16). If the saints were "on their feet" and as eager to obey the Lord as sinners are to disobey, the lost world would soon be evangelized!

God has called His people to be witnesses to the truth (Acts 1:8), but the wicked person is *a false witness who speaks lies.* Bearing false witness is a violation of the Ninth Commandment (Ex. 20:16). Without truth, things start to fall apart; when people "lie officially," the foundations of society begin to crumble. Whether it's a statement from a government official, a clause in a contract, a deposition in court, or a promise at the marriage altar, truth cannot be violated without society ultimately suffering. The British poet John Dryden wrote, "Truth is the foundation of all knowledge and the cement of all societies."

The last of the seven sins that God hates is *sowing discord among brethren.* "Behold, how good and how pleasant it is for brethren to dwell together in unity" (Ps. 133:1). The wicked person destroys that unity by sowing "seeds" that produce a bitter and divisive harvest. Some of these seeds are: pride (Prov. 13:10; see 3 John 9-10), gossip (Prov. 16:28; 17:9; 18:8; 26:20), anger and hatred (10:12; 15:18; 29:22), a quarrelsome spirit (17:14, 19; 25:8; 26:21), and foolish questions (1 Tim. 6:3-5; 2 Tim. 2:14, 23).

The truly godly person sows seeds of unity and peace, not

seeds of division (James 3:17-18). Discord and division in the church are terrible sins because they are contrary to the spiritual unity that Jesus prayed for (John 17:21) and that the Spirit was given to produce in the body (Eph. 4:1-6). How can lost sinners ever believe that God loves *them* when God's children don't even love *one another?*

All it takes is one stubborn troublemaker to wreck the unity in a family, a Bible study group, or a church. "Drive out the mocker, and out goes strife; quarrels and insults are ended" (Prov. 22:10, niv). In one of the churches I pastored, we had such a man. When the Lord finally removed him, the new atmosphere in the fellowship was exhilarating. Official meetings that used to consume hours were considerably shortened, and there was a new freedom in discussion and decision.

It is enlightening to contrast this description of the wicked person with Christ's description of the godly person in Matthew 5:1-16. Jesus begins with humility, "the poor in spirit" (Matt. 5:3), while Solomon starts with "a proud look" (Prov. 6:17). "When pride comes, then comes shame; but with the humble is wisdom" (11:2). The seventh characteristic of the wicked is sowing discord among brethren, while the seventh beatitude is "Blessed are the peacemakers" (Matt. 5:9).

There is a wisdom from above that brings peace and purity to God's people, and there is a wisdom from beneath that brings strife and shame (James 3:13-18). There is a wisdom of this world that destroys the church and a wisdom from God that builds the church (1 Cor. 3:16-23).

"To the law and to the testimony! If they do not speak according to this word, it is because there is no light in them" (Isa. 8:20, nkjv).

SIX

People, Wise and Otherwise — Part 2 (The Simple, Scorner, and Fool)

While much more could be said about both the wise and the wicked, we need to move on and get better acquainted with "the terrible trio" — the simple, the scorners, and the fools. You will meet these three frequently as you read the Book of Proverbs.

You'll recall that in her first invitation, Wisdom called to all three of them (Prov. 1:22), but in her second invitation, she called only to the simple and the fools (8:5). The scorner wasn't even interested in listening; he had dropped out of the picture. Then, in her third invitation, Wisdom called only to the simple (9:4), because the fools had turned away and joined the scorners. *It's a dangerous thing to reject God's invitation to walk the path of wisdom and of life. You may never get another opportunity.*

1. The simple

The simple are the naive people who believe everything, because they don't have convictions about anything. What they think is sophisticated "tolerance" is only spiritual ignorance, because they lack the ability to discriminate between truth and error. "A simple man believes anything, but a prudent man gives thought to his steps" (14:15, NIV). Charles R. Bridges writes, "To *believe every word* of God is faith. To *believe every word* of man is credulity."[1]

We're living at a time when people who have convictions are considered bigots if not ignoramuses. It's popular and politically correct to be open-minded and uncritical of what other people think or believe. Except when it comes to cashing a check when they're broke, getting a prescription filled when they're sick, or asking directions when they're lost, most people don't believe in absolutes. They insist that there's no such thing as objective truth. According to them, whatever "feels good" down inside is truth for you; nobody has the right to criticize you for what you believe. Apply that philosophy to money, medicine, mechanics, or maps and see how successful you will be!

In his comments on "Groundhog's Day," Brooks Atkinson writes: "People everywhere enjoy believing things they know are not true. It spares them the ordeal of thinking for themselves and taking responsibility for what they know."[2] The old saying, "What you don't know won't hurt you," is false, as any physician or auto mechanic can tell you. What you don't know could kill you! "For the turning away [waywardness] of the simple shall slay them" (1:32).

The simple are simple because they reject the truth of God's Word that gives "prudence [common sense] to the simple" (v. 4, NIV). The tragedy is that simple people actually love their simplicity (v. 22) and have no desire to change. Because they don't take a stand for anything, they fall for everything; this saves them the trouble of thinking, studying, praying, and asking God for wisdom. Instead of working hard to dig into the mines of God's wisdom (2:1-9), the simple prefer to take it easy and pick up whatever cheap trinkets they can find on the surface.

It was a simple young man who listened to the prostitute

and ended up an animal led to the slaughter (7:7ff). "The simple inherit folly, but the prudent are crowned with knowledge" (14:18). Sometimes the simple will learn when they see others punished for their sins (19:25; 21:11). The wise person learns from instruction, but the simpleton has to see a living example before he or she will learn. Wise people see danger coming and avoid it, but the simple ones walk right into it (22:3; 27:12). Some people have to learn the hard way.

All of us are ignorant in many things, but simpletons are ignorant of their ignorance and are unwilling to learn. They follow the philosophy, "Where ignorance is bliss, 'tis folly to be wise."[3] But when there's a Bible to read, a life to build, and an eternity to prepare for, it is folly to be ignorant.

2. The scorner

Scorners think they know everything, and anybody who tries to teach them is only wasting time. "Proud and haughty scorner [scoffer] is his name" (21:24). Scorners can't find wisdom even if they seek for it (14:6), because learning God's truth demands a humble mind and an obedient will. What scorners lack in knowledge they make up for in arrogance. Instead of sensibly discussing a matter with those who could teach them, they only sneer at truth and deny it. My Hebrew lexicons describe them as "frivolous and impudent." Having no intellectual or spiritual ammunition, the scorner depends on ridicule and contempt to fight his enemies.

Scorners show how ignorant they are by the way they respond to advice and reproof. "He who reproves a scoffer gets shame for himself. . . . Do not reprove a scoffer, lest he hate you; rebuke a wise man, and he will love you" (9:7-8, NKJV). "A wise son heeds his father's instruction, but a scoffer does not listen to rebuke" (13:1, NKJV). "A scoffer does not love one who corrects him, nor will he go to the wise" (15:12, NKJV). When you try to teach a scorner, you're just casting pearls before swine. The scorner knows everything!

The tragedy is that scorners cause all kinds of trouble wherever they go. Whether in the neighborhood, on the job, or in the church, the scorner is toxic and spreads infection. "Cast out the scorner, and contention shall go out; yea, strife and reproach shall cease" (22:10). Scorners can even create problems for a whole city. "Mockers [scorners] stir up a city, but wise men turn away anger" (29:8, NIV). The Hebrew verb translated "stir up" conveys the image of somebody stirring up a fire or blowing on a flame to make it burn more vigorously. By their contemptible words and attitudes, they add fuel to a fire that ought to be allowed to die out.

The pages of both religious and political history are stained by the records of the deeds of proud mockers who wouldn't listen to wise counsel but impulsively rushed into matters too high for them (Ps. 131). Their tongues were "set on fire of hell" (James 3:6); they defiled and damaged families, churches, cities, and entire nations. Churches can be quickly divided and destroyed by arrogant people who laugh at biblical truth and seek to have their own way. All spiritual leaders need to read and heed Acts 20:28-31 and James 3:13-18.

Scoffers are "an abomination to men" (Prov. 24:9) and to God. In fact, the Lord "scorns the scornful, but gives grace to the humble" (3:34, NKJV). This verse is quoted both by James (4:6) and Peter (1 Peter 5:5). "Judgments are prepared for scoffers" (Prov. 19:29), and because scorners mock God, God mocks the scorners. Consider what the Lord did to the builders at Babel (Gen. 11), to Pharaoh at the Red Sea (Ex. 14), to Nebuchadnezzar in Babylon (Dan. 4), and to Herod Agrippa in Judea (Acts 12:20-25), and a host of others who defied His will.

3. The fool

The English words "fool" and "folly" come from the Latin *follis*, which means "bellows." It also described a person's puffed-up cheeks. *Follis* indicates that a fool is a windbag, somebody full of air but lacking in substance. Fools may look like giants, but when the wind is taken out of them, they shrink dramatically and reveal what they really are—pygmies.

In Proverbs, three different Hebrew words are translated "fool": *kesyl,* the dull, stupid fool who is stubborn; *ewiyl,* the corrupt fool who is morally perverted and unreasonable; and *nabal,* the fool who is like a stubborn animal, the brutish fool. (See 1 Sam. 25.) In this summary of the characteristics of the fool, we'll combine the verses and not distinguish the three different types. After all, fools are fools, no matter what name we give them!

Fools won't learn from God's Word. "The fear of the Lord is the beginning [controlling principle] of knowledge: but fools despise wisdom and instruction" (1:7). The problem with fools isn't low IQ or deficient education. Their big problem is their heart: They won't acknowledge the Lord and submit to Him. "There is no fear of God before their eyes" (Rom. 3:18).

A fool's own father can't instruct him (Prov. 15:5), and if you try to debate with him, it will only lead to trouble (29:9). Why? Because fools actually enjoy their folly and think they're really living! "Folly is a joy to him who is destitute of discernment" (15:21, NKJV; see 1:22; 12:15; 18:2). Warn them about sin and they laugh at you (14:9).

One reason fools don't learn wisdom is because they can't keep their eyes focused on what's important. "A discerning man keeps wisdom in view, but a fool's eyes wander to the ends of the earth" (17:24, NIV). Instead of dealing with reality, the fool lives in a faraway fantasy world. God's Word helps people keep their feet on the ground and make wise decisions in this difficult world in which we live.

Fools can't control their speech. "The tongue of the wise uses knowledge rightly, but the mouth of fools pours forth foolishness" (15:2, NKJV; see 13:16). The fool's speech is proud and know-it-all (14:3), and fools have a tendency to speak before they know what they're saying or what's being discussed (18:13). "Do you see a man hasty in his words? There is more hope for a fool than for him" (29:20, NKJV). "The way of a fool is right in his own eyes, but he who heeds counsel is wise" (12:15, NKJV). You can't warn fools or tell them anything they need to know because they already know everything!

Fools do a lot of talking, but they never accomplish what they've talked about. "The wise in heart will receive commandments: but a prating fool shall fall" (10:8; see v. 10). The word translated "prating" means "to babble and talk excessively," and is related to the word "prattle." It's much easier to talk about things than to hear God's Word and obey it.

Lies and slander are what fools specialize in (10:18), and the wise person won't stay around to listen (14:7-8). "The lips of the wise disperse knowledge, but the heart of the fool does not do so" (15:7, NKJV). "Excellent speech is not becoming to a fool" (17:7, NKJV). All of us must be careful what kind of conversation we listen to, because Jesus said, "Take heed what you hear" (Mark 4:24). Furthermore, when fools are speaking, what they say could start a fight! (18:6-7)

Fools can't control their temper. "A fool's wrath is known at once, but a prudent man covers shame" (12:16, NKJV). "He who is slow to wrath has great understanding, but he who is impulsive exalts folly" (14:29, NKJV). "Even a fool is counted wise when he holds his peace; when he shuts his lips, he is considered perceptive" (17:28, NKJV). "A fool vents all his feelings, but a wise man holds them back" (29:11, NKJV).

When business is being transacted in the city gate (Ruth 4), fools should keep quiet if they want to appear wise! (Prov. 24:7) It's unfortunate that some people think they must always speak at meetings, even when they have nothing to say.

Don't incur the wrath of a fool unless you want to carry a terrible burden. "A stone is heavy, and the sand weighty, but a fool's wrath is heavier than them both" (27:3). Once a fool is angry with you, he or she will carry on the war to the bitter end and do a great deal of damage. That's why we must exercise discernment when we disagree with fools or try to counsel them. "Do not answer a fool according to his folly, or you will be like him yourself. Answer a fool according to his folly, or he will be wise in his own eyes" (26:4-5, NIV). Sometimes fools deserve only a deaf ear; other times they must be rebuked and their folly answered from the Word. It takes wisdom to know which response is correct, lest we end up casting pearls before swine.

Fools are proud and self-confident. "He who trusts in his own heart is a fool, but whoever walks wisely will be delivered" (28:26, NKJV). "Do you see a man wise in his own eyes? There is more hope for a fool than for him" (26:12). We hear people saying, "Well, if I know my own heart . . ." but God warns us that we don't know our own hearts and we can't always trust what our hearts say to us. "The heart is deceitful above all things, and desperately wicked; who can know it?" (Jer. 17:9)

Many people today believe what Emerson wrote: "Trust thyself: every heart vibrates to that iron string."[4] Or they may follow William Ernest Henley's philosophy as expressed in his famous poem, "Invictus": "I am the master of my fate/I am the captain of my soul." These expressions of proud human achievement sound very much like Satan's offer in Eden: "You will be like God" (Gen. 3:5, NKJV), which is the basis of the New Age movement. Whatever exalts man will ultimately fail; whatever glorifies God will last forever.[5]

Because of their proud self-confidence, fools like to meddle, especially when there's something to argue about: "It is an honor for a man to cease from strife: but every fool will be meddling" (Prov. 20:3). Anybody can start a quarrel, but it takes a wise person to be able to stop one or, better yet, to avoid one (30:32-33). Fools think that fighting over minor disagreements will bring them honor, but it only makes them greater fools.

While waiting for a Sunday morning worship service to begin at a church where I was to be the guest preacher, I sat in an adult Sunday School class that met in the church sanctuary. One man in that class questioned almost everything the teacher said and really made a nuisance of himself quibbling about minor things. He wanted to appear wise, but he only convinced us that he was a fool. As I sat there listening, I thought of 1 Timothy 6:4-5: "He is proud, knowing nothing, but is obsessed with disputes and arguments over words, from which come envy, strife, reviling, evil suspicions, useless wranglings" (NKJV).

Fools create problems and bring sorrow, especially to their parents. "A wise son makes a glad father, but a foolish son is the grief of his mother" (Prov. 10:1, NKJV; see 15:20; 17:21, 25). Every godly father says to his son, "Be wise, my son, and bring joy to my heart" (27:11, NIV), but the pages of the Bible record the sorrow that foolish sons brought to their parents.

Cain grieved his parents when he killed his brother Abel (Gen. 4). Esau deliberately married heathen women just to provoke his father Isaac (Gen. 28:6-9). Jacob's sons lied to him about their brother Joseph and broke his heart (Gen. 37). Samson grieved his parents by living with pagan women and fraternizing with the enemies of Israel (Jud. 13–16). David's sons broke his heart with their evil ways. Amnon violated his half sister Tamar and Absalom killed him for doing it (2 Sam. 13). Then Absalom rebelled against David and seized the kingdom (2 Sam. 15–18).

Can anything be done to change foolish children into wise

men and women? "Though you grind a fool in a mortar, grinding him like grain with a pestle, you will not remove his folly from him" (Prov. 27:22, NIV). Women in the ancient world ground grain in a bowl (mortar) using a hard tool (pestle) with which they could crack and pulverize the kernels. The image is clear: no amount of pressure or pain will change a fool and make anything useful out of him. Wise parents should discipline foolish children to give them hope (22:15),[6] but a foolish adult can be changed only by the grace of God. Unless fools repent and turn to the Lord, they will live as slaves (11:29) and "die without instruction" (5:23).

Fools don't know how to use wealth properly. "In the house of the wise are stores of choice food and oil, but a foolish man devours all he has" (21:20, NIV). Fools may know the price of everything, but they know the value of nothing; they waste their wealth on things stupid and sinful. "Whoever loves wisdom makes his father rejoice, but a companion of harlots wastes his wealth" (29:3, NKJV). This verse reminds us of our Lord's Parable of the Prodigal Son (Luke 15:11-24). "The crown of the wise is their riches, but the foolishness of fools is [yields] folly" (Prov. 14:24). The wise have something to leave to their children, but fools waste both their wealth and their opportunities to increase it. "Luxury is not fitting for a fool" (19:10).

Fools can't be trusted with responsibility. "As snow in summer and rain in harvest, so honor is not fitting for a fool" (26:1, NKJV). The word *honor* in the Hebrew *(kabod)* means "heavy, weighty," and can refer to the glory of God and the special respect given to people. A fool doesn't have what it takes to handle responsibility successfully and win the respect of others. Giving honor to a fool is about as fitting as snow in summer or as helpful as rain during harvest! Both mean disaster.

In 26:3-12, Solomon elaborates on this theme by presenting a number of vivid pictures of the fool and what happens when you give him a job to do. For one thing, you'll have to treat him like a dumb animal and use a whip to motivate him (v. 3; see Ps. 32:9). Try to give him orders and explain what he's to do and you're in danger of becoming like him (Prov. 26:4-5). Send him on an important mission and you might as well cripple yourself, and be prepared for trouble (v. 6).[7] As a lame person's legs are useless to take him anywhere, so a fool can't "get anywhere" with a proverb (v. 7). He not only confuses others, but he harms himself, like a drunk punctured by a thorn (v. 9). Don't ask a fool to teach the Bible because he won't know what he's talking about and it's painful to listen to him. And don't ask a fool to wage war because he ties the stone in the sling! (v. 8)

The original text of verse 10 is very difficult and there are many varied translations. "Like an archer who wounds everyone, so is he who hires a fool or who hires those who pass by" (NASB). "Like an archer who wounds at random is he who hires a fool or any passer-by" (NIV). "Like an archer who wounds everybody is he who hires a passing fool or drunkard" (RSV). Note that the emphasis is on the one doing the hiring and not on the fool. If you hire a fool (or just anybody who passes by) and give him or her responsibility, you might just as well start shooting at random, because the fool will do a lot of damage. Of course, nobody in his right mind would start shooting at random, so, nobody in his right mind would hire a fool.

Fools don't learn from their mistakes but go right back to the same old mess, like a dog returning to eat his vomit (v. 11). Experience is a good teacher for the wise, but not for fools. This verse is quoted in 2 Peter 2:22 as a description of counterfeit believers who follow false teachers. Like a sow that's been washed, they look better on the outside; and like a dog that's vomited, they feel better on the inside; but they're still not sheep! They don't have the divine new nature; consequently, they go right back to the old life. Obedience and perseverance in the things of the Lord are proof of conversion.

What will happen to the fool? "A man's own folly ruins his life, yet his heart rages against the Lord" (Prov. 19:3, NIV). This reminds us of Pharaoh in Exodus 5–15, who saw his country ruined by God's plagues and yet wouldn't give in to the Lord. He raged against Jehovah and Moses and even pursued the Jews to take them back, only to see his best soldiers drowned in the Red Sea. God's discipline helps a wise person obey the Word, but punishment only makes a foolish person more wicked. The same sun that melts the ice hardens the clay.

Because they "feed on foolishness" (Prov. 15:14), fools have no moral strength. "The lips [words] of the righteous feed many, but fools die for lack of wisdom" (10:21). They not only lack spiritual and intellectual nourishment, but they also lack refreshing water: "Understanding is a fountain of life to those who have it, but folly brings punishment to fools" (16:22, NIV). The image of words and God's Law as "a fountain of life" is also found in 10:11; 13:14; 14:27, and 18:4. Follow Wisdom and you live on a fruitful oasis; follow Folly and your home is an arid desert.

The fool will "die without instruction" (5:23). "The wise shall inherit glory: but shame shall be the promotion of fools" (3:35). They will hear God's voice say, "Fool! This night your soul will be required of you" (Luke 12:20, NKJV), but then it will be too late.

The only fools who are "wise fools" are Christians, because they're 'fools for Christ's sake" (1 Cor. 4:10). The world calls them fools, but in trusting Jesus Christ and committing their lives to Him, they've made the wisest decision anybody can make.

BE SKILLFUL

I read about a man who bore witness to his faith in a busy shopping area by wearing a sandwich board which read:
I'M A FOOL FOR JESUS CHRIST.
WHOSE FOOL ARE YOU?
A wise question! Be sure you can give a wise answer.

SEVEN

"Rich Man, Poor Man, Beggar Man, Thief"

M oney isn't everything," said a wit, "but it does keep you in touch with your children."

On a more serious level, Paul summarized the Christian philosophy of wealth when he wrote: "Let him who stole steal no longer, but rather let him labor, working with his hands what is good, that he may have something to give him who has need" (Eph. 4:28, NKJV).

According to Paul, you can get wealth in three ways: by stealing it, earning it, or receiving it as a gift, which would include getting it as an inheritance. Stealing is wrong (Ex. 20:15), labor is honorable (Ex. 20:9) and, "It is more blessed to give than to receive" (Acts 20:35).

In the Book of Proverbs, King Solomon tells us a great deal about these three kinds of people—the thieves, the workers, and the poor who need our help. (Among the thieves, I'm including "the sluggard," the lazy person who never works but expects others to take care of him. That's being a thief, isn't it?) However, wealthy as he was (1 Kings 4; 10), King Solomon emphasized that *God's wisdom is more important than money.* "How much better is it to get wisdom than gold! and to get understanding rather to be chosen than silver!"

(Prov. 16:16; see 2:1-5; 3:13-15; 8:10-21) This is Solomon's version of Matthew 6:33; he's reminding us that while it is good to have the things money can buy, be sure you don't lose the things money can't buy.

1. The thieves

The Book of Proverbs opens with a stern warning against participating in get-rich-quick schemes that involve breaking the Law (Prov. 1:10-19). These schemes are self-destructive and lead to bondage and possibly the grave. Beware of people who promise to make you wealthy without asking you to work or take any risks. "Wealth obtained by fraud dwindles, but the one who gathers by labor increases it" (13:11, NASB). "A man with an evil eye hastens after riches, and does not consider that poverty will come upon him" (28:22, NKJV). "Ill-gotten treasures are of no value, but righteousness delivers from death" (10:2, NIV).

Proverbs 21:5-7 points out three ways *not* to get wealth: following hasty schemes (v. 5), lying to people (v. 6), and robbing (v. 7). Most if not all get-rich-quick schemes involve some kind of deception and are nothing but scams.[1] Unfortunately, even God's people have been duped by scam artists, and more than one trusting soul has lost his or her life savings in a "sure thing" that turned out to be a sure loser. However, scams wouldn't succeed if there weren't people eager to get rich as quickly and easily as possible. But, as the old adage puts it, "There are no free lunches." You take what you want from life, but eventually you pay for it.

God demands that we be honest in all our business dealings. Dishonesty is robbery. "Dishonest scales are an abomination to the Lord, but a just weight is His delight" (11:1, NKJV; see 16:11; 20:10, 23). Moses commanded in the Law that the people use honest weights and measures (Lev. 19:35-36; Deut. 25:13-16); since Israel didn't have an official

Department of Standards to check on these things, the law wasn't always obeyed. Amos accused the merchants in his day of "skimping the measure, boosting the price and cheating with dishonest scales" (Amos 8:5, NIV); Micah asked, "Shall I count them pure with the wicked balances, and with the bag of deceitful weights?" (Micah 6:11)

Another dishonest way to get wealth is to use your resources selfishly and disregard the needs of others. "A generous man will prosper; he who refreshes others will himself be refreshed. People curse the man who hoards grain, but blessing crowns him who is willing to sell" (Prov. 11:25-26, NIV). In times of drought and famine, a prosperous farmer could corner the grain market and become rich at the expense of his needy neighbors (see Neh. 5). We need to realize that everything we have comes from God (1 Cor. 4:7; John 3:27) and that we are but stewards of His wealth. While everyone expects that a businessman will make a profit, nobody wants him to "make a killing" and hurt others.

The biggest thieves of all are the lazy people who could work but won't, the people who consume what others produce but produce nothing for others to use. The "sluggard" and the "slothful man" are mentioned at least seventeen times in Proverbs, and nothing good is said about them.

We need to recognize the fact that *work is not a curse*. God gave Adam work to do in the Garden even before sin entered the scene (Gen. 2:15). Before He began His public ministry, Jesus worked as a carpenter (Mark 6:3); the Apostle Paul was a tentmaker (Acts 18:1-3). In that day, rabbis had vocations and supported themselves but didn't accept payment from their students. When we engage in honorable employment, we're cooperating with God in caring for and using His creation, we're helping to provide for others, and we're growing in character. The work God has called us to do ought to nourish us (John 4:34), not tear us down; "the laborer is worthy of his hire" (Luke 10:7; 1 Tim. 5:18).

What are some of the marks of sluggards? For one thing, *they love to sleep.* "How long will you lie there, you sluggard? When will you get up from your sleep?" (Prov. 6:9, NIV) "As a door turns on its hinges, so does the lazy man on his bed" (26:14). Lots of motion—but no progress!

Sleep is a necessary element for a healthy life, but too much sleep is destructive. Wise people enjoy sleep that's "sweet" (3:24) because they know they're in God's will, and the laborer's sleep is "sweet" because he or she has worked hard (Ecc. 5:12), but the sleep of the sluggard is a mark of selfishness and laziness. "Laziness could run a competitive race for the most underrated sin," write Ronald Sailler and David Wyrtzen in *The Practice of Wisdom* (Chicago: Moody, 1992). "Quietly it anesthetizes its victim into a lifeless stupor that ends in hunger, bondage and death" (p. 82).

Put the sluggard to work and *he's more of a nuisance than a help.* "As vinegar to the teeth, and as smoke to the eyes, so is the sluggard to them that send him" (Prov. 10:26). Vinegar on the teeth and smoke in the eyes aren't necessarily lethal, but they do irritate you; so does a sluggard who won't get the job done. All he does is dream about the things he wants to enjoy, but he won't work hard enough to earn them. "The sluggard's craving will be the death of him, because his hands refuse to work" (21:25, NIV). Dreams become nightmares if you don't discipline yourself to work.

Another mark of the sluggard is a *know-it-all attitude.* "The lazy man is wiser in his own eyes than seven men who can answer sensibly" (26:16, NKJV). He lives in a fantasy world that prevents him from being a useful part of the real world (13:4; 21:25-26), but he can tell everybody else what to do. He's never succeeded at anything in his own life, but he can tell others how to succeed.

Sluggards are good at *making excuses.* Either the weather

is too cold for plowing (20:4) or it's too dangerous to go out of the house (22:13; 26:13). "The way of the sluggard is blocked with thorns, but the path of the upright is a highway" (15:19, NIV). The diligent man or woman can always find a reason to work, but the sluggard always has an excuse for not working. Evangelist Billy Sunday defined an excuse as, "the skin of a reason stuffed with a lie," and he was right. People who are good at making excuses are rarely good at doing anything else.

What finally happens to the sluggard? For one thing, unless others care for them, *sluggards live in poverty and hunger.* "Laziness casts one into a deep sleep, and an idle person will suffer hunger" (19:15, NKJV; see 10:4; 13:4). "If any would not work, neither should he eat" was the standard for the New Testament church (see 2 Thes. 3:6-15). The saints were happy to care for those who needed help and couldn't care for themselves, but they had no time for freeloaders who lived by the sacrifices of others (Acts 2:44-47; 1 Tim. 5:3-16). The sluggard gets so lazy, he won't feed himself even when the food is brought right to him! (Prov. 19:24; 26:15)

The sluggard *loses his freedom and is enslaved to others.* "The hand of the diligent will rule, but the lazy man will be put to forced labor" (12:24, NKJV). His debts accumulate to the point where he has to become a slave and work off what he owes (see Lev. 25:39-55; Deut. 15:12-18). The "easy life" of leisure turns out to be very costly as the sluggard exchanges his pillow for a plow and has to work off his debts the hard way.

The sluggard *wastes God-given resources.* "He also that is slothful in his work is brother to him that is a great waster" (Prov. 18:9). The lazy person may be "working" but not doing a very good job. Consequently, what's done will either have to be thrown out or done over; this means it will cost twice as much.

The sluggard also wastes *God-given opportunities.* "He who gathers in summer is a wise son; he who sleeps in harvest is a son who causes shame" (10:5, NKJV). When the fields are ready for harvest, the reapers have to go to work, because the opportunity won't be there forever (John 4:27-38). Diligent people are alert to their God-given opportunities and seek to make the most of them.

2. The poor and needy

Had the nation of Israel obeyed God's laws, their land would have remained fruitful and there would have been very little poverty or oppression of the poor. Every seventh day was a Sabbath, when the people rested and gave their land and farm animals rest. Every seventh year was a Sabbatical Year, when the land and workers were allowed to rest for the entire year. Every fiftieth year was a Year of Jubilee, when the land not only lay fallow but was returned to its original owners (Lev. 25:1-34). By this means, the Lord sought to restore the fertility of the land regularly and also prevent wealthy people from amassing huge farms and thus controlling the economy. According to 2 Chronicles 36:20-21, the nation didn't obey these special laws for the land; God had to send the people to Babylon to give the land a rest.

What are the causes of poverty and need? Some people are poor simply because they won't work. Work is available but they prefer not to know about it. "Lazy hands make a man poor, but diligent hands bring wealth" (Prov. 10:4, NIV). "Do not love sleep, lest you come to poverty" (20:13, NKJV). Or perhaps the enemy is pleasure: "He who loves pleasure will be a poor man; he who loves wine and oil will not be rich" (21:17, NKJV). Of course, the drunkard and the glutton are usually among the poor (23:21). Time, energy, money, and opportunity are wasted when leisure and pleasure control a person's life.

Unfortunately, some people weren't disciplined when young and taught the importance of work. "He who ignores discipline comes to poverty and shame, but whoever heeds correction is honored" (13:18, NIV). Listening to orders and obeying them, paying attention to correction and reproof and not repeating mistakes, and respecting supervision are essential to success in any job. It's worth noting that the Prodigal's first request was, "Father, give me!" But when he returned home, his desire was, "Make me one of your servants" (Luke 15:12, 19). He'd learned the value of his father's discipline and the joy of hard work.

Some people are needy because *they like to talk but never act.* "In all labor there is profit, but idle chatter leads only to poverty" (Prov. 14:23, NKJV). This reminds us of our Lord's parable about the two sons (Matt. 21:28-32).

People can become poor because of *unwise financial dealings.* Rush impulsively into a "good deal" and you may lose everything (Prov. 21:5), and beware of signing notes and assuming other people's debts (6:1-5), especially strangers (11:15). "A man devoid of understanding shakes hands in a pledge, and becomes surety for his friend" (17:18, NKJV; see 22:26-27). The Jews were permitted to loan money to other Jews, but they were not to charge interest (Lev. 25:35-38; Ex. 22:25). They were permitted to charge interest to Gentiles (Deut. 23:20). However, they were warned against "going surety" and assuming debts larger than they could pay (Prov. 22:7).

There are also times when people become poor because of *people and events over which they have no control.* "A poor man's field may produce abundant food, but injustice sweeps it away" (13:23, NIV; see 18:23; 28:8). The prophets condemned wicked rulers and businessmen who crushed the poor and seized what little they had (Isa. 3:13-15; 10:1-4; Amos 2:6-7; 4:1; 5:11-12; 8:4-10). When there's justice in the land and people fear the Lord, then the poor have a voice and protection from oppression.

Oppressing the poor is condemned by God. "He who oppresses the poor reproaches his Maker, but he who honors Him has mercy on the needy" (Prov. 14:31, NKJV). God doesn't respect the rich more than He respects the poor. "The rich and the poor have this in common, the Lord is the maker of them all" (22:2, NKJV). The poor are made in the image of God, so the way we treat the poor is the way we treat God. Churches that show deference to the rich and ignore the poor have forgotten the royal law, "Thou shalt love thy neighbor as thyself" (James 2:1-8).

How do we help the poor? To begin with, we ought not to look down on the poor because of their troubles, thinking we are better than they. "He who despises his neighbor sins; but he who has mercy on the poor, happy is he" (Prov. 14:21, NIV). God has a special concern for the poor and needy, and in exploiting them we will find ourselves fighting the Lord. "Rob not the poor, because he is poor: neither oppress the afflicted in the gate: for the Lord will plead their cause, and spoil [plunder] the soul of those that spoiled them" (22:22-23; see Deut. 15:7; 24:12).

Christian citizens ought to see to it that laws are written fairly and enforced justly. "The righteous care about justice for the poor, but the wicked have no such concern" (Prov. 29:7, NIV). "A ruler who oppresses the poor is like a driving rain that leaves no crops" (28:3, NIV). "Speak up and judge fairly; defend the rights of the poor and needy" (31:9, NIV). "The king who judges the poor with truth, his throne will be established forever" (29:14). These are solemn statements indeed!

When we assist the poor, we are investing with the Lord, and He will see to it that we get our dividends at the right time.[2] "He who has pity on the poor lends to the Lord, and

He will pay back what he has given" (19:17; see 11:24; 22:9). Before the church helps, however, the family has an obligation to assist their own needy (1 Tim. 5:4, 8). This leaves the church free to help those who have no one to share their burdens. If we shut our ears to the cries of the poor, God will shut His ears to our prayers (Prov. 21:13).

Having pastored three churches, I know some of the problems congregations can have with "con artists" who pose as "believers passing through town who need help." In over forty years of ministry, I recall very few instances when strangers we helped wrote and thanked us when they got home or even repaid the gift. Certainly pastors and deacons must exercise caution and wisdom lest they do more harm than good, but we must also remember that we're helping truly needy people for Jesus' sake (Matt. 25:34-40). Bernard of Clairvaux, composer of "Jesus, the Very Thought of Thee," gave wise counsel when he said, "Justice seeks out the merits of the case, but pity only regards the need." If our Lord dealt with us today only on the basis of justice, where would we be?

3. The diligent

Diligent hands are directed by a diligent heart, and this means *the discipline of the inner person.* "Keep your heart with all diligence, for out of it springs the issues of life" (Prov. 4:23, NKJV). When we cultivate the inner person through prayer, meditation on the Word, and submission to the Lord, then we can experience the joys of a disciplined and diligent life. "The fruit of the Spirit is . . . self-control" (Gal. 5:22-23).

The reward for faithful hard work is—more work! "Well done, good and faithful servant; you were faithful over a few things, I will make you ruler over many things" (Matt. 25:21, NKJV; see Luke 19:16-19). "Do you see a man who excels in his work? He will stand before kings; he will not stand before unknown men" (Prov. 22:29, NKJV).

One of the blessings of diligent labor is the joy of developing the kind of ability and character that others can trust, thereby fitting ourselves for the next responsibility God has prepared for us. Joseph was faithful in suffering and service, and this prepared him to rule Egypt. David faithfully cared for a few sheep, and God gave him an entire nation to shepherd (Ps. 78:70-72). Joshua was faithful as Moses' helper and became Moses' successor. "Wisdom is the principal thing. . . . Exalt her, and she will promote you" (Prov. 4:7-8, NKJV). "The wise shall inherit glory: but shame shall be the promotion of fools" (3:35).

There's no substitute for hard work. "Lazy hands make a man poor, but diligent hands bring wealth" (10:4, NIV). "All hard work brings a profit, but mere talk leads only to poverty" (14:23, NIV). A new college graduate was asked if he was looking for work. He thought for a minute and then replied, "No, but I would like to have a job." That seems to be the attitude of too many people today. Poet Robert Frost said, "The world is full of willing people: some willing to work and the rest willing to let them."

Diligent people *plan their work and work their plan.* "The plans of the diligent lead surely to plenty, but those of everyone who is hasty, surely to poverty" (21:5, NKJV). "Commit your works to the Lord, and your thoughts will be established" (16:3, NKJV; see 24:27). Thomas Edison said, "I never did anything worth doing by accident, nor did any of my inventions come by accident; they came by work." More than one scientific breakthrough seemed to be discovered by accident, but there was still a great deal of hard work put into the project before the breakthrough came. Benjamin Franklin wrote in his *Poor Richard's Almanack,* "Diligence is the mother of good luck, and God gives all things to industry."

RICH MAN, POOR MAN, BEGGAR MAN, THIEF

God blesses the labors of people who are *honest*. "Wealth gained by dishonesty will be diminished, but he who gathers by labor will increase" (13:11, NKJV). God expects "a just weight and a just balance" (16:11; see 20:10, 23). He also expects us to be honest in our words as we deal with people in our work. "Lying lips are an abomination to the Lord, but those who deal truthfully are His delight" (12:22, NKJV).

God blesses diligent people for their *generosity*. "There is one who scatters, yet increases more; and there is one who withholds more than is right, but it leads to poverty. The generous soul will be made rich, and he who waters will also be watered himself" (11:24-25, NKJV). "He who has a generous eye will be blessed, for he gives of his bread to the poor" (22:9, NKJV). Mark the difference between the diligent worker and the slothful person: "The desire of the lazy man kills him, for his hands refuse to labor. He covets greedily all day long, but the righteous gives and does not spare" (21:25-26, NKJV).

Diligent people are *careful not to incur debts they can't handle*. "The rich rules over the poor, and the borrower is servant to the lender" (22:7, NKJV). While a certain amount of honest debt is expected in today's world, and everybody wants to achieve a good credit rating, we must be careful not to mistake presumption for faith. As the familiar adage puts it, "When your outgo exceeds your income, then your upkeep is your downfall."

It's a dangerous thing for people to become greedy for more and more money and to overextend themselves to acquire it. Each of us must discover at what financial level God wants us to live and be content with it. "Two things I ask of you, O Lord; do not refuse me before I die: Keep falsehood and lies far from me; give me neither poverty nor riches, but give me only my daily bread. Otherwise, I may have too much and disown You and say, 'Who is the Lord?' Or I may become poor and steal, and so dishonor the name of my God" (30:7-9, NIV).

I was a "depression baby" and the text my sister and two brothers and I learned to live by was, "Use it up, wear it out; make it do, or do without." Our parents taught us the difference between luxuries and necessities, and they didn't try to impress the neighbors by purchasing things they didn't need with money they couldn't afford to spend. But that philosophy of life seems to have almost disappeared. Today if you talk about hard work, wise stewardship, the dangers of debt, and the importance of accountability before God, somebody is bound to smile (or laugh out loud) and tell you that times have changed.

Our Heavenly Father knows that His children have needs that must be met (Matt. 6:32); in our modern society, this means we must have money to procure them. But our most important task isn't to earn money; our most important task is to be the kind of people God can trust with money, people who are faithful in the way we use what God gives us. "But seek first the kingdom of God and His righteousness, and all these things shall be added to you" (Matt. 6:33, NKJV).

"The real measure of our wealth," said John Henry Jowett, "is how much we'd be worth if we lost all our money." Character is more important than position, and wisdom than possessions. God doesn't glorify poverty, but neither does He magnify affluence. "There is one who makes himself rich, yet has nothing; and one who makes himself poor, yet has great riches" (Prov. 13:7, NKJV).

We must not think that the way of the wealthy is always easy,[3] because there are also perils that accompany wealth and success in life. Wealthy people face problems that people of ordinary means don't face, for an increase in wealth usually means an increase in decision-making, risk-taking, and possibly physical danger. "A man's riches may ransom his life, but a poor man hears no threat" (13:8, NIV). Kenneth Taylor aptly paraphrases this verse, "Being kidnapped and held for ransom never worries the poor man!" (TLB) Thieves will break into a mansion but not a hovel.

One of the subtle dangers of wealth is *a false sense of security.* "He who trusts in his riches will fall, but the righteous will flourish like foliage" (11:28). After all, riches won't save the sinner on the day of judgment (11:4); they can't buy peace (15:16-17) or a good name (22:1). Riches have a tendency to fly away when we least expect it (23:4-5; 27:23-24).

If God blesses our diligent work with success, *we must be careful not to become proud.* "The wealth of the rich is their fortified city; they imagine it an unscalable wall" (18:11, NIV). This reminds us of the rich farmer in our Lord's parable (Luke 12:13-21). If successful people aren't careful, they'll start mistreating people (Prov. 14:21; 18:23) and becoming a law to themselves (28:11). "By humility and the fear of the Lord are riches, and honor, and life" (22:4). Rich people have many friends (14:20; 19:4, 6), but will those friends remain faithful if the rich become poor? (19:7) Wealth is a wonderful servant for humble people but a terrible master for the proud.

The wrong attitude toward money can *wreck friendships and even destroy a home.* "He who is greedy for gain troubles his own house, but he who hates bribes will live" (15:27, NKJV). The man or woman who thinks only of getting rich will put money ahead of people and principles, and soon they start to neglect the family in their frantic pursuit of wealth. Expensive gifts to the children become substitutes for the gift of themselves; before long, values become twisted and the family falls apart. How many families have been destroyed because of the distribution of an estate! As a lawyer friend of mine used to say, "Where there's a will, there's relatives."

In connection with that problem, wealthy people have to worry about *what their children will do with their wealth.* "For riches are not forever, nor does a crown endure to all generations" (27:24, NKJV). Solomon discussed this problem in Ecclesiastes 2:18-26 and came to the conclusion that the best thing rich people can do is enjoy their wealth while they're able and not worry about their heirs. Perhaps their will should read, "Being of sound mind and body, I spent it all!"[4]

"Rich man, poor man, beggar man, thief." God has a word for all of them. Are they willing to receive it?

EIGHT

Family, Friends, and Neighbors

In 1937, the number one fiction bestseller in the United States was Margaret Mitchell's *Gone with the Wind.* The number one nonfiction title was Dale Carnegie's *How to Win Friends and Influence People,* and since then, millions of copies have been sold around the world. Why? Because just about everybody has "people problems" and wants to know how to solve them. Getting along with other people is an important part of life.

The Book of Proverbs is the best manual you'll find on people skills, because it was given to us by the God who made us, the God who can teach us what we need to know about human relationships, whether it's marriage, the family, the neighborhood, the job, or our wider circle of friends and acquaintances. If we learn and practice God's wisdom as presented in Proverbs, we'll find ourselves improving in people skills and enjoying life much more.

1. Husbands and wives

According to Scripture, God established three human institutions in the world: marriage and the home (Gen. 2:18-25), human government (Gen. 9:1-6; Rom. 13), and the local church (Acts 2); of the three, the basic institution is the home. As goes the home, so go the church and the nation. The biblical views of marriage and the family have been so attacked and ridiculed in modern society that it does us good to review what the Creator of the home has to say about His wonderful gift of marriage.

Marriage. King Solomon had 700 wives and 300 concubines (1 Kings 11:3), and in so doing he disobeyed God's Law — by multiplying wives (Deut. 17:17), and by taking these wives from pagan nations that didn't worship Jehovah, the true and Living God (Ex. 34:16; Deut. 7:1-3). Eventually, these women won Solomon over to their gods, and the Lord had to discipline Solomon for his sins (1 Kings 11:4ff).

In contrast to this, the Book of Proverbs magnifies the kind of marriage that God first established in Eden: one man married to one woman for one lifetime (Gen. 2:18-25; Matt. 19:1-9).[1] The husband is to love his wife and be faithful to her (Prov. 5). The wife is not to forsake her husband and seek her love elsewhere (2:17). They are to enjoy one another and grow in their love for each other and for the Lord.

In ancient days, marriages were arranged by the parents. Our modern "system" of two people falling in love and getting married would be foreign to their thinking and their culture. In that day, a man and woman got married and then learned to love each other; they expected to stay together for life. Today, a man and woman learn to love each other, then they get married, and everybody hopes they'll stay together long enough to raise the children.

The husband. A man can inherit houses and lands, but "a prudent wife is from the Lord" (19:14, NIV).[2] "He who finds a wife finds a good thing, and obtains favor from the Lord" (18:22, NKJV). Blessed is that marriage in which the husband acknowledges God's goodness to him in giving him his wife! When a husband takes her for granted, he grieves both her and the Lord. He should love her and be loyal to her all the days of his life.

The Book of Proverbs places on the husband the responsibility of guiding the home according to the wisdom of God, but as we shall see in chapter 31, the wife also plays an important part. Where two people love the Lord and love each other, God can guide and bless them. It's not a "fifty-fifty" arrangement, because "two become one." Rather, it's a 100 percent devotion to each other and to the Lord.

The wife. Every wife will either build the home or tear it down (14:1). If she walks with the Lord, she will be a builder; if she disobeys God's wisdom, she will be a destroyer. She must be faithful to her husband, for "A wife of noble character is her husband's crown, but a disgraceful wife is like decay in his bones" (12:4, NIV). A crown or a cancer: What a choice! And beauty isn't the only thing he should look for; it's also important that a wife have wisdom and discretion (11:22).

Husbands occasionally create problems for their wives, but Solomon doesn't mention any of them. However, he does name some of the problems a wife might create for her husband. "The contentions of a wife are a continual dropping" (19:13). A wife who quarrels constantly creates the kind of atmosphere in a home that would tempt her husband to look for attention elsewhere. "Better to live on the corner of a roof than share a house with a quarrelsome wife" (21:9, NIV; see 21:19; 25:24; 27:15-16). But let's be fair and admit that the situation might be reversed and the husband be the culprit. God hates family discord (6:19), and we should do everything we can to practice in the home the kind of love that produces unity and harmony.

The finest description of the ideal wife is found in 31:10-31. This poem is an acrostic with the initial words of the twenty-two verses all beginning with successive letters of the Hebrew alphabet (see Ps. 119). This acrostic form was a device to help people commit the passage to memory. Perhaps Jewish parents instructed their sons and daughters to memorize this poem and use it as a guide for their lives and in their homes. What kind of wife is described here?

First of all, *she is a woman of character* (Prov. 31:10-12). Just as wisdom is more important than wealth (3:15), so character is more important than jewels. Peter gave this same counsel to Christian wives in his day (1 Peter 3:1-6). *Marriage doesn't change a person's character.* If there are character weaknesses in either the husband or the wife, marriage will only reveal and accentuate them. A husband or wife who hopes to change his or her spouse after the honeymoon is destined for disappointment.

If the husband and wife trust each other, there will be harmony in the home. Her husband has no fears or suspicions as she is busy about her work, because he knows she has character and will do nothing but good for him and their children. If brides and grooms take seriously the vows of love and loyalty they repeat to each other and to God at the altar, they will have a wall of confidence around their marriage that will keep out every enemy.

She's a woman *who isn't afraid to work* (Prov. 31:13-22, 24). Whether it's going to the market for food (vv. 14-15), buying real estate (v. 16a), or planting a vineyard (v. 16b), she's up early and busy with her chores. You get the impression that the night before she makes a list of "things to do" and doesn't waste a minute in idleness. "She sets about her work vigorously" (v. 17, NIV), whether spinning thread, helping the poor, or providing a wardrobe for her children. She prepares the very best for her family and they have no reason to be ashamed.

She is a *generous* person (v. 20). As she ministers to her family, she keeps her eyes open for people who have needs, and she does what she can to help them. Happiness comes to those who have mercy on the poor (14:21), and nothing given to the Lord for them will ever be lost (19:17).

This wife *makes it easy for her husband to do his work* (v. 23). The city gate was the place where civic business was transacted, so her husband was one of the elders in the community (Ruth 4). While no such restrictions exist today, it would have been unthinkable in that day for a woman to sit on the "city council." But this loyal wife didn't want to take his place; she just did her work and made it easier for him to do his.

A husband and wife should complement each other as they each seek to fulfill their roles in the will of God. Wise is that husband who recognizes his wife's strengths and lets her compensate for his weaknesses. Doing this isn't a sign of personal failure, nor is it rebellion against the divine order (1 Cor. 11:3). Both leadership and submission in a home are evidences of love and obedience, and the one doesn't nullify the other.

She is confident as she faces the future (Prov. 31:25). In the Bible, to be "clothed" with something means that it is a part of your life and reveals itself in your character and conduct. (See 1 Tim. 2:9-10; Col. 3:8-14.) This wife can laugh at future problems and troubles because she has strength of character and she's prepared for emergencies. She is a woman of faith who knows that God is with her and her family.

This wife is a capable *teacher of wisdom* (Prov. 31:26). She certainly teaches her children the wisdom of God, especially the daughters, preparing them for the time when they will have homes of their own. But it's likely that she also shares her insights with her husband, and he's wise enough to listen. Remember that earlier in the book, Solomon used a beautiful woman to personify wisdom; this godly wife does the same.

She is an *attentive overseer of the household* (v. 27). She isn't idle, and nothing in the household escapes her notice, whether it's food, finances, clothing, or school lessons. Managing the household is an exacting job, and she does her work faithfully day and night. Any husband and father who thinks that his wife "has it easy" should take her responsibilities for a week or two and discover how wrong he is!

She's a woman *worthy of praise* (vv. 28-29). It's a wonderful thing when husband and children can praise wife and mother for her faithful ministry in the home. The suggestion here is that this praise was expressed regularly and spontaneously and not just on special occasions. (They didn't have Mother's Day in Israel. Every day should be Mother's Day and Father's Day!) It's tragic when the members of a family take each other for granted and fail to show sincere appreciation. The father ought to set the example for the children and always thank his wife for what she does for the family. He should see in her the woman who surpasses them all!

The secret of her life is that she *fears the Lord* (v. 30). It's wonderful if a wife has charm and beauty; the possession of these qualities is not a sin. But the woman who walks with the Lord and seeks to please Him has a beauty that never fades (1 Peter 3:1-6). The man who has a wife who daily reads the Word, meditates, prays, and seeks to obey God's will, has a treasure that is indeed beyond the price of rubies.

Finally, *her life is a testimony to others* (Prov. 31:31). Her husband and children acknowledge her value and praise her, but so do the other people in the community. Even the leaders in the city gate recognize her good works and honor her. "A kindhearted woman gains respect" (11:16, NIV). God sees to it that the woman who faithfully serves Him and her family is properly honored, and certainly she will have even greater honor when she stands before her Lord.

This beautiful tribute to the godly wife and mother tells

every Christian woman what she can become if she follows the Lord. It also describes for every Christian man the kind of wife for whom he ought to be looking and praying. But it also reminds the prospective husband that he'd better be walking with the Lord and growing in his spiritual life so that he will be worthy of such a wife if and when God brings her to him.

2. Parents and children

In ancient Israel, a Jewish husband and wife would no more consider aborting a child than they would consider killing each other. Their philosophy was, "Behold, children are a heritage from the Lord, the fruit of the womb is a reward" (Ps. 127:3). To them, marriage was a "bank" into which God dropped precious children who were His investment for the future, and it was up to the father and mother to raise those children in the fear of God. Children were rewards not punishments, opportunities not obstacles. They aren't burdens; they're investments that produce dividends.

Along with the basic necessities of physical life, what should the godly home provide for the children?

Example. "The righteous man leads a blameless life; blessed are his children after him" (Prov. 20:7, NIV), and we've already considered the influence of the godly mother's example (31:28). British statesman Edmund Burke called example "the school of mankind," and its first lessons are learned in the home even before the children can speak. Benjamin Franklin said that example was "the best sermon," which suggests that the way parents act in the home teaches their children more about God than what the children hear in Sunday School and church.

When parents walk with God, they give their children a heritage that will enrich them throughout their lives. Godliness puts beauty within the home and protection around the home. "He who fears the Lord has a secure fortress, and for his children it will be a refuge" (14:26, NIV). The world wants to penetrate that fortress and kidnap our children and grandchildren, but godly parents keep the walls strong and the spiritual weapons ready.

Instruction. "My son, hear the instruction of your father, and do not forsake the law of your mother" (1:8, NKJV; 6:20). The Book of Proverbs is primarily the record of a father's instructions to his children, instructions that they were to hear and heed all their lives. "Cease listening to instruction, my son, and you will stray from the words of knowledge" (19:27, NKJV). "My son, keep my words, and treasure my commands within you" (7:1, NKJV).

The man who deliberately walked into the trap of the adulteress did so because he ignored what his parents had taught him. "How I have hated instruction, and my heart despised correction! I have not obeyed the voice of my teachers, nor inclined my ear to those who instructed me!" (5:12-13) As we get older, it's remarkable how much more intelligent our parents and teachers become!

The Bible is the basic textbook in the home. It was once the basic textbook in the educational system, but even if that were still true, the Bible in the school can't replace the Bible in the home. I note that many modern parents sacrifice time and money to help their children excel in music, sports, and social activities; I trust they're even more concerned that their children excel in knowing and obeying the Word of God.

Every parent should pray and work so that their children will have spiritual wisdom when the time comes for them to leave the home. "A wise son makes a glad father, but a foolish son is the grief of his mother" (10:1, NKJV; see 15:20; 23:15-16, 24-25; 27:11; 29:3). "A wise son heeds his father's instruction, but a scoffer does not listen to rebuke" (13:1, NKJV). In my pastoral ministry, I have often had to share the grief of parents and grandparents whose children and grandchildren turned their backs on the Word of God and the godly example given in the home. In some instances, the children, like the Prodigal Son, "came to themselves" and returned to the Lord, but they brought with them memories and scars that would torture them for the rest of their lives.

Loving discipline. Many modern educators and parents revolt against the biblical teaching about discipline. They tell us that, "Spare the rod and spoil the child" is nothing but brutal prehistoric pedagogy that cripples the child for life.[3] But nowhere does the Bible teach blind brutality when it comes to disciplining children. The emphasis is on love, because this is the way God disciplines His own children. "My son, do not despise the chastening of the Lord, nor detest His correction; for whom the Lord loves He corrects, just as a father the son in whom he delights" (3:11-12, NKJV; 13:24). Do we know more about raising children than God does?

Discipline has to do with correcting character faults in a child while there is still time to do it (22:15). Better the child is corrected by a parent than by a law enforcement officer in a correctional institution. "Chasten your son while there is hope, and do not set your heart on his destruction" (19:18, NKJV). I prefer the NIV translation of the second clause: "do not be a willing party to his death." A vote against discipline is a vote in favor of premature death. (See 23:13-14.)

What a tragedy when children are left to themselves, not knowing where or what the boundaries are and what the consequences of rebellion will be! I may be wrong, but I have a suspicion that many people who can't discipline their children have a hard time disciplining themselves. If you want to enjoy your children all your life, start by lovingly disciplining them early. "The rod and rebuke give wisdom, but a child left to himself brings shame to his mother" (29:15, NKJV). "Correct your son, and he will give you rest; yes, he will give delight to your soul" (29:17, NKJV).

Proverbs 22:6 is a religious "rabbit's foot" that many sorrowing parents and grandparents desperately resort to when children stray from the Lord: "Train up a child in the way he should go: and when he is old, he will not depart from it." They interpret this to mean, "they will stray away for a time but then come back," but that isn't what it says. It says that if they're raised in the wisdom and way of the Lord, *they won't stray away at all.* Even in old age, they will follow the wisdom of God.

Certainly it's true that children raised in the nurture and admonition of the Lord can stray from God, but they can never get away from the prayers of their parents or the seed that's been planted in their hearts. Parents should never despair but keep on praying and trusting God to bring wayward children to their senses. But that isn't what Proverbs 22:6 is speaking about. Like the other proverbs, it's not making an ironclad guarantee but is laying down a general principle.[4]

In the autumn of 1993, we replaced a pin oak that a tornado had ripped out of our front yard, and the nursery people attached three guy-wires to the trunk of the new tree to make sure it would grow straight. They also taped metal rods to two limbs that were growing down instead of straight out. If you don't do these things while the tree is young and pliable, you'll never be able to do it at all. "As the twig is bent, so is the tree inclined," says an old proverb, a paraphrase of Proverbs 22:6.

God has ordained that parents are older and more experienced than their children and should therefore lovingly guide their children and prepare them for adult life. If any of their children end up sluggards (10:5), gluttons (28:7), fornicators (29:3), rebels (19:26; 20:20; 30:11-12, 17; see Deut. 21:18-21) and robbers (28:24), it should be *in spite of* the parents' training and not *because of* it.

3. Friends and neighbors

G.K. Chesterton said that God commanded us to love both our enemies and our neighbors because usually they were the same people. My wife and I have always been blessed with wonderful neighbors whom we consider friends; that seems to be the biblical ideal, for the Hebrew word *(ra'a)* can mean "friend" or "neighbor." In this survey, we'll include both meanings; for what's true of friends ought to be true of neighbors.

The basis for friendship. Proverbs makes it clear that true friendship is based on love, because only love will endure the tests that friends experience as they go through life together. "A friend loves at all times, and a brother is born for adversity" (17:17, NKJV). It's possible to have many companions and no real friend. "A man of many companions may come to ruin, but there is a friend who sticks closer than a brother" (18:24, NIV). Friendship is something that has to be cultivated and its roots must go deep.

God's people must be especially careful in choosing their friends. "The righteous should choose his friends carefully, for the way of the wicked leads them astray" (12:26, NKJV). "He who walks with wise men will be wise, but the companion of fools will be destroyed" (13:20). Friendships that are based on money (6:1-5; 14:20; 19:4, 6-7) or sin (16:29-30; 1:10-19) are destined to be disappointing. So are friendships with people who have bad tempers (22:24-25), who speak foolishly (14:7), who rebel against authority (24:21-22, NIV), or who are dishonest (29:27). Believers need to heed Psalm 1:1-2 and 2 Corinthians 6:14-18.

The qualities of true friendship. I've already mentioned *love*, and true love will produce *loyalty*. "A friend loves at all times" (Prov. 17:17, NIV) and "there is a friend who sticks closer than a brother" (18:24, NIV). Sometimes our friends do more for us in an emergency than our relatives do! By the way, this loyalty ought to extend to our parents' friends. "Do not forsake your friend and the friend of your father" (27:10, NIV). Long-time family friends can be a blessing from one generation to the next.

True friends know how to *keep a confidence.* "If you argue your case with a neighbor, do not betray another man's confidence, or he who hears it may shame you and you will never lose your bad reputation" (25:9-10, NIV). If you have a disagreement with somebody, don't bring another person into the discussion by betraying confidence, because you'll end up losing both your reputation ("You can't trust him with anything confidential!") and your friend who trusted you with his private thoughts. "A gossip betrays a confidence, but a trustworthy man keeps a secret" (11:13, NIV; see 20:19). If we aren't careful, gossip can ruin a friendship (16:28), so the wise thing to do is to cover offenses with love (17:9; 1 Peter 4:8).

This leads to the next important quality for true friends and good neighbors: *the ability to control the tongue.* "With his mouth the godless destroys his neighbor, but through knowledge the righteous escape" (Prov. 11:9, NIV). Don't believe the first thing you hear about a matter, because it may be wrong (18:17); remember that "a man of understanding holds his tongue" (11:12, NIV). If your neighbor or friend speaks falsely of you, talk to him about it privately, but don't seek to avenge yourself by lying about him (24:28-29; 25:18). And beware of people who cause trouble and then say, "I was only joking" (26:18-19).

Friends and neighbors must be *lovingly honest with one another.* "Faithful are the wounds of a friend; but the kisses of an enemy are deceitful" (27:6). True friendship in the Lord can't be built on deception; even if "the truth hurts," it can never harm if it's given in love. Better that we "speak the truth in love" (Eph. 4:15), because the Spirit can use truth and love to build character, while the devil uses lies and flattery to tear things down (Prov. 29:5). "He who rebukes a man will find more favor afterward than he who flatters with the tongue" (28:23). It has well been said that flattery is manipulation, not communication; what honest person would want to manipulate a friend?

We must never take our friends for granted and think that they will immediately forgive our offenses, even though forgiveness is the right thing for Christians. "A brother offended is harder to win than a strong city, and contentions are like the bars of a castle" (18:19). It's strange but true that some of God's people will forgive offenses from unbelievers that they would never forgive if a Christian friend committed them. It takes a diamond to cut a diamond, and some Christians have a way of putting up defenses that even the church can't break through. Matthew 18:15-35 gives us the steps to take when such things happen, and our Lord warns us that an unforgiving spirit only puts us into prison!

Faithful friends and neighbors *counsel and encourage each other.* "Ointment and perfume delight the heart, and the sweetness of a man's friend gives delight by hearty counsel" (Prov. 27:9, NKJV). The images of oil and perfume are fine when the discussion is pleasant, but what's it like when friends disagree? "As iron sharpens iron, so a man sharpens the countenance of his friend" (27:17). If we're not disagreeable, we usually learn more by disagreeing than by giving in and refusing to say what we really think, "speaking the truth in love" (Eph. 4:15).

Friends and neighbors must *exercise tact and be sensitive to each other's feelings.* If we spend too much time together, we may wear out our welcome. "Seldom set foot in your neighbor's house, lest he become weary of you and hate you" (Prov. 25:17, NKJV). I've known people who spent so much time with each other that they eventually destroyed their friendship. If we're going to grow, we need space; space comes from privacy and solitude. Even husbands and wives must respect each other's privacy and not be constantly together if their love is to mature.

"He who blesses his friend with a loud voice, rising early in the morning, it will be counted a curse to him" (27:14, NKJV). Beware the "friend" who loudly and frequently praises you and tells you what a good friend you are, because true friendship doesn't depend on such antics—especially if he wakes you up to do it! Love is sensitive to other people's feelings and needs, and true friends try to say the right thing at the right time in the right way (25:20).

A happy family, encouraging friends, and good neighbors: What blessings these are from the Lord! Let's be sure we do our part to make these blessings a reality in our lives and the lives of others.

NINE

A Matter of Life or Death
(Human Speech)

A judge speaks some words and a guilty prisoner is taken to a cell on death row. A gossip makes a phone call and a reputation is blemished or perhaps ruined. A cynical professor makes a snide remark in a lecture and a student's faith is destroyed.

Never underestimate the power of words. For every word in Hitler's book *Mein Kampf,* 125 people died in World War II.[1] Solomon was right: "Death and life are in the power of the tongue" (Prov. 18:21). No wonder James compared the tongue to a destroying fire, a dangerous beast, and a deadly poison (James 3:5-8). Speech is a matter of life or death.

When you summarize what Proverbs teaches about human speech, you end up with four important propositions: (1) speech is an awesome gift from God; (2) speech can be used to do good; (3) speech can be used to do evil; and, (4) only God can help us use speech to do good.

1. Speech is an awesome gift from God

Our older daughter's first complete sentence was, "Where Daddy go?" Considering how full my schedule was in those days, it was an appropriate question for her to ask. But, who taught Carolyn how to understand and speak those words? And who explained to her how to put together a sentence that asked a question?

"The ability [to speak] comes so naturally that we are apt to forget what a miracle it is," writes Professor Steven Pinker. "Language is not a cultural artifact that we learn the way we learn to tell time or how the federal government works. Instead, it is a distinct piece of the biological makeup of our brains."[2] Christian believers would say that when God created our first parents, He gave them the ability to speak and understand words. Made in the image of a God who communicates, human beings have the wonderful gift of speech. "The answer of the tongue is from the Lord" (16:1).

God spoke to Adam and gave him instructions about life in the Garden, which he later shared with Eve; they both understood what God told them (Gen. 2:15-17; 3:2-3). Adam was able to name the animals (2:18-20) and to give a descriptive name to his bride (vv. 22-24). Satan used words to deceive Adam and Eve (3:1-5), and Eve must have used words to persuade her husband to eat (v. 6). The Garden of Eden was a place of communication because God gave Adam and Eve the ability to understand and use words.

The images used in Proverbs for human speech indicate the value of this divine gift that we not only take for granted but too often waste and abuse. Wise words are compared to *gold and silver.* "The tongue of the just is like choice silver: the heart of the wicked is little worth" (Prov. 10:20). "A word aptly spoken is like apples of gold in settings of silver. Like an earring of gold or an ornament of fine gold is a wise man's rebuke to a listening ear" (25:11-12, NIV). Our words ought to be as balanced, beautiful, and valuable as the most precious jewelry; we ought to work as hard as the craftsman to make them that way. (See Ecc. 12:9-11.)

Words are also like *refreshing water.* "The mouth of a righteous man is a well [fountain] of life" (Prov. 10:11). "The words of a man's mouth are deep waters; the wellspring of wisdom is a flowing brook" (18:4, NKJV). When we listen to and appropriate the words of a godly person, it's like taking a drink of refreshing water. "The law of the wise is a fountain of life" (13:14) and "the fear of the Lord is a fountain of life" (14:27). But it isn't enough for the wise to speak to us; we must be prepared to listen. "Understanding is a wellspring of life to him who has it" (16:22, NKJV). The soil of the heart must be prepared and the seed of the Word planted, or the water won't do us much good.

Right words are like *nourishing, health-giving food.* "The tongue that brings healing is a tree of life, but a deceitful tongue crushes the spirit" (15:4, NIV). What a wonderful thing it is to say the right words and help to heal a broken spirit! The phrase, "tree of life," means "source of life" and goes back to Genesis 2:9.[3] "The lips of the righteous feed many" (Prov. 10:21; see 18:20). "Pleasant words are like a honey-comb, sweetness to the soul and health to the bones" (16:24, NKJV; see Ps. 119:103). "Reckless words pierce like a sword, but the tongue of the wise brings healing" (Prov. 12:18, NIV; see 12:14; 13:2).

The Apostle Paul considered biblical doctrine to be "healthy doctrine" ("sound doctrine," KJV)[4] that nourishes the believer's spiritual life. He warned Timothy to beware of anything that was "contrary to sound [healthy] doctrine" (1 Tim. 1:10), and he reminded him that the time would come when professed Christians wouldn't "endure sound [healthy] doctrine" (2 Tim. 4:3). Spiritual leaders are to use sound doctrine to exhort the careless and rebuke the deceivers (Titus 1:9-10; 2:1). The words of Jesus are "wholesome [healthy] words," but the words of false teachers are "sick" (1 Tim. 6:3-4, see NIV). "Their teaching will spread like gangrene" (2 Tim. 2:17, NIV), but God's words are "life to those who find them, and health to all their flesh" (Prov. 4:22, NKJV).

The Christian who recognizes how awesome is the gift of speech will not abuse that gift but will dedicate it to the glory of God. The New Testament scholar Bishop B.F. Westcott wrote, "Every year makes me tremble at the daring with which people speak of spiritual things." We all need to heed the words of Solomon: "Do not be rash with your mouth, and let not your heart utter anything hastily before God. For God is in heaven, and you on earth; therefore let your words be few" (Ecc. 5:2, NKJV).

2. Speech can be used to do good

No matter what may be wrong with us physically, when the doctor examines us, he or she often says, "Stick out your tongue!" This principle applies to the Christian life, for what the tongue does reveals what the heart contains. Inconsistent speech bears witness to a divided heart, for it is "out of the abundance of the heart" that the mouth speaks (Matt. 12:34). "Out of the same mouth proceedeth blessing and cursing," wrote James. "My brethren, these things ought not so to be" (James 3:10).

What we say can help or hurt other people. When we reviewed some of the images of speech found in Proverbs, we learned that our words can bring beauty and value, nourishment, refreshment, and healing to the inner person. But the awesome power of words reveals itself in other positive ways.

Our words can bring peace instead of war. "A soft [gentle] answer turns away wrath, but a harsh word stirs up anger" (Prov. 15:1, NKJV). "A hot-tempered man stirs up dissension, but a patient man calms a quarrel" (v. 18, NIV).[5] Solomon isn't advising us to compromise the truth and say that what's wrong is really right. Rather, he's counseling us to have a gentle spirit and a conciliatory attitude when we disagree with others. This can defuse the situation and make it easier for us to settle the matter peacefully.

Once again, the key issue is the condition of the heart. If there's war in the heart, then our words will be destructive missiles instead of healing medicines. "But if you have bitter envy and self-seeking in your hearts, do not boast and lie against the truth" (James 3:14, NKJV). Earthly wisdom advises us to fight for our rights and make every disagreement a win/lose situation, but heavenly wisdom seeks for a win/win situation that strengthens the "unity of the Spirit in the bond of peace" (Eph. 4:3). "But the wisdom that is from above is first pure, then peaceable, gentle, willing to yield,[6] full of mercy and good fruits, without partiality and without hypocrisy" (James 3:17, NKJV). Applying this wisdom means taking the attitude that's described in Philippians 2:1-12, the attitude that was practiced by Jesus Christ.

Our words can help restore those who have sinned. "As an earring of gold, and an ornament of fine gold, so is a wise reprover upon an obedient [listening] ear" (Prov. 25:12). It isn't easy to reprove those who are wrong, and we need to do it in a meek and loving spirit (Gal. 6:1); yet it must be done. To flatter those who are disobeying God's Word will only confirm them in their sin and make us their accomplices. "He who rebukes a man will find more favor afterward than he who flatters with the tongue" (28:23, NKJV). "He who keeps instruction is in the way of life, but he who refuses reproof goes astray" (10:17, NKJV).

In Matthew 18:15-20 Jesus explains the procedure for helping restore a sinning brother or sister. First, we must talk to the offender personally and confidentially, trusting God to change the heart. If that fails, we must try again, this time taking witnesses with us. If even that fails, then what was confidential must become public as we share the matter with the church. If the offender fails to hear the church, then he or she must be excluded from the church as though they were not believers at all. Of course, during this whole procedure, we must be much in prayer, seeking the Lord's help for ourselves and for those we're trying to help.

Our words can instruct the ignorant. "The lips of the wise disperse knowledge" (Prov. 15:7). "The wise in heart are called discerning, and pleasant words promote instruction" (16:21, NIV). While there are many good and helpful things to learn in this brief life that we have on earth, the most important is the wisdom of God found in the Word of God (8:6-8). "Wisdom is the principal thing; therefore get wisdom. And in all your getting, get understanding" (4:7, NKJV). After we acquire wisdom, we must share it with others, for "wisdom is found on the lips of the discerning" (10:13, NIV).

Whether it's parents teaching their children (Deut. 6:1-13), older women teaching the younger women (Titus 2:3-5), or spiritual leaders in the church teaching the next generation of believers (2 Tim. 2:2), accurate instruction is important to the ongoing of the work of God. Every local church is but one generation short of extinction; if we don't teach the next generation the truth of God, they may not have a church.

In spite of all the books and periodicals that are published and all the Christian programs that are broadcast, we're facing today a famine of God's Word (Amos 8:11). People attend church services and special meetings of all kinds, purchase Bibles and books, and listen to Christian radio and TV. But there seems to be little evidence that all this "learning" is making a significant difference in families, churches, and society as a whole. Many professed believers are "spiritually illiterate" when it comes to the basics of the Christian life. We desperately need men who will obey 2 Timothy 2:2 and women who will obey Titus 2:3-5, or we will end up with an uninstructed church.

Our words can rescue the perishing. "A true witness delivers souls, but a deceitful witness speaks lies" (Prov. 14:25, NKJV). While this verse can be applied to our own personal witness for Christ in rescuing the lost (Acts 1:8), the context is that of a court of law. An accused criminal in Israel could be condemned on the testimony of two or three witnesses; if the case involved a capital crime, the witnesses had to be the first to cast the stones (Deut. 17:6-7). The law forbade the bearing of false witness (Ex. 20:16; 23:2; Deut. 5:20), and anyone found guilty of perjury was given the punishment that the accused would have received (Deut. 19:16-18).

If my testimony could save an innocent person from death, and I refused to speak, then my silence would be a terrible sin. "Deliver those who are drawn toward death, and hold back those stumbling to the slaughter. If you say, 'Surely we did not know this,' does not He who weighs the hearts consider it? He who keeps your soul, does He not know it? And will He not render to each man according to his deeds?" (Prov. 24:11-12, NKJV) Whether it's rescuing prisoners from execution or lost sinners from eternal judgment, we can't plead ignorance if we do nothing.

Our words can encourage those who are burdened. "Anxiety in the heart of man causes depression, but a good word makes it glad" (12:25, NKJV). "A man finds joy in giving an apt reply—and how good is a timely word!" (15:23, NIV) When we're walking in the Spirit daily and being taught by the Lord, we'll know how "to speak a word in season to him who is weary" (Isa. 50:4). "Pleasant words are a honeycomb, sweet to the soul and healing to the bones" (Prov. 16:24, NIV).

The Royal British Navy has a regulation which reads, "No officer shall speak discouragingly to another officer in the discharge of his duties." We need to practice that regulation in our homes and churches! Each of us needs to be a Barnabas, a "son of encouragement" (Acts 4:36-37). Near the close of his ministry, a famous British preacher of the Victorian Age said, "If I had my ministry to do over, I would preach more to broken hearts." Jesus came, "to heal the broken-hearted" (Luke 4:18), and we can continue that ministry today with words of encouragement and hope.

3. Speech can be used to do evil

From Satan's speech to Eve in Genesis 3 to the propaganda of the false prophet in the Book of Revelation, the Bible warns us that words can be used to deceive, control, and destroy. It is estimated that the average American is exposed to over 1,500 "promotion bites" in the course of a day, some of them subliminal and undetected, but all of them powerful. Whether it's political "double-speak,"[7] seductive advertising, or religious propaganda, today's "spin doctors" know how to manipulate people with words.

But it isn't only some of the professional promoters who are guilty. There are many ways that you and I can turn words into weapons and damage others.

We hurt others by lying. "Truthful lips endure forever, but a lying tongue lasts only a moment" (Prov. 12:19, NIV). "Lying lips are an abomination to the Lord, but they that deal truly are His delight" (12:22; and see 6:16-17). Solomon warns us against bearing false witness and violating the Ninth Commandment (Ex. 20:16). See Proverbs 14:5, 25; 19:5, 9, 28; 21:28; 24:28. When words can't be trusted, then society starts to fall apart. Contracts are useless, promises are vain, the judicial system becomes a farce, and all personal relationships are suspect. "Like a club or a sword or a sharp arrow is the man who gives false testimony against his neighbor" (25:18, NIV).

One of the marks of liars is that they enjoy listening to lies. "A wicked man listens to evil lips; a liar pays attention to a malicious tongue" (17:4, NIV). It's a basic rule of life that the ears hear what the heart loves, so beware of people who have an appetite for gossip and lies.

"An honest answer is like a kiss on the lips" (24:26, NIV; see 27:6). A kiss is a sign of affection and trust, and God wants His people to "[speak] the truth in love" (Eph. 4:15). It has well been said that love without truth is hypocrisy and truth without love is brutality, and we don't want to be guilty of either sin. The world affirms, "Honesty is the best policy," but as the British prelate Richard Whateley said, "He who acts on that principle is not an honest man." We should be honest because we're honest people in our hearts, walking in the fear of the Lord, and not because we're shrewd bargainers who follow a successful policy.

We hurt others by gossiping. "You shall not go about as a talebearer among your people" (Lev. 19:16, NKJV). "Talebearer" is the translation of a Hebrew word that means "to go about," and is probably derived from a word meaning "merchant." The talebearer goes about peddling gossip! "A talebearer reveals secrets, but he who is of a faithful spirit conceals a matter" (Prov. 11:13, NKJV). Gossips flatter people by sharing secrets with them, but to be one of their "customers" is dangerous. "He who goes about as a talebearer reveals secrets; therefore do not associate with one who flatters with his lips" (20:19, NKJV).

The gossip "eats" and enjoys his secrets like you and I eat and enjoy food. "The words of a gossip are like choice morsels; they go down to a man's inmost parts" (18:8, NIV; see 26:22). People who feed on gossip only crave more, and the only remedy is for them to develop an appetite for God's truth (2:10). We must beware of gossips because they do a great deal of damage. "An ungodly man digs up evil, and it is on his lips like a burning fire. A perverse man sows strife, and a whisperer separates the best of friends" (16:27-28,

NKJV; see 17:9). "Where there is no wood, the fire goes out; and where there is no talebearer, strife ceases" (26:20, NKJV).

We hurt others by flattery. The English word "flatter" comes from a French word that means "to stroke or caress with the flat of the hand." Flatterers compliment you profusely, appealing to your ego, but their praise is far from sincere. They pat you on the back only to locate a soft spot in which to stick a knife! "A man who flatters his neighbor spreads a net for his feet" (29:5, NKJV).

"A lying tongue hates those who are crushed by it, and a flattering mouth works ruin" (26:28, NKJV). Satan flattered Eve when he said, "You shall be as God" (Gen. 3:5). In Proverbs, the prostitute seduces her prey by using flattery (Prov. 5:3; 7:5, 21). Some people flatter the rich because they hope to get something from them (14:20; 19:4, 6).

Most of us secretly enjoy flattery and dislike rebuke, yet rebuke does us more good (27:6; 28:23). There is certainly a place for honest appreciation and praise, to the glory of God (1 Thes. 5:12-13), but we must beware of people who give us insincere praise with selfish motives, especially if they begin their flattery first thing in the morning (Prov. 26:24-25). If it weren't for our pride, flattery wouldn't affect us. We privately enjoy hearing somebody agree with what we think of ourselves!

We hurt others by speaking in anger. "An angry man stirs up dissension, and a hot-tempered one commits many sins" (29:22, NIV). Angry people keep adding fuel to the fire (26:21) instead of trying to find ways to put the fire out. Many people carry anger in their hearts while they outwardly pretend to be at peace with their friends, and they cover their anger with hypocritical words. "Fervent lips with a wicked heart are like earthenware covered with silver dross" (26:23, NKJV). If we're inwardly angry at people, all our profuse professions of friendship are but a thin veneer over common clay. "Speak when you are angry," wrote Ambrose Bierce, "and you will make the best speech you will ever regret."

Instead of covering our anger with cheap dross, we should cover others' sins with sincere love. "Hatred stirs up strife, but love covers all sins" (10:12, NKJV; 1 Peter 4:8). Love doesn't *condone* sin or encourage sinners to try to hide their sins from the Lord (Prov. 28:13; 1 John 1:9), but love doesn't tell the sin to others. (See Gen. 9:18-29.) If I'm angry with someone and he sins, I'll be tempted to spread the news as a way of getting even.

We hurt others by impetuous speech. "Do you see a man hasty in his words? There is more hope for a fool than for him" (Prov. 29:20, NKJV). "He who answers a matter before he hears it, it is folly and shame to him" (18:13, NKJV; note v. 17). "The heart of the righteous studies how to answer, but the mouth of the wicked pours forth evil" (15:28, NKJV; see 10:19). "Reckless words pierce like a sword" (12:18, NIV). But reckless words not only hurt others, they can also hurt us because we utter them. "Whoever guards his mouth and tongue keeps his soul from troubles" (21:23, NKJV; see 13:3). This is especially true when we make rash promises to the Lord or to others (20:25; 22:26-27; see Ecc. 5:1-5).

We hurt others by talking too much. "In the multitude of words sin is not lacking, but he who restrains his lips is wise" (Prov. 10:19, NKJV). "The mouth of fools pours forth foolishness" (15:2). People who discipline their tongue can control their whole body (James 3:1-2). There is "a time to keep silence, and a time to speak" (Ecc. 3:7), and the wise know how to hold their peace (Prov. 11:12-13; 17:28).

We hurt others by talking instead of working. "All hard work brings a profit, but mere talk leads only to poverty" (14:23, NIV). Mankind seems to be divided into three classes: *dreamers* who have great ideas but never accomplish much, *talkers* who exercise their jaw muscles and vocal cords but not their hands and feet, and *doers* who talk little but with God's help turn their dreams into realities.

4. Only God can help us use the gift of speech for good
When David prayed, "Set a watch, O Lord, before my mouth; keep the door of my lips" (Ps. 141:3), he was doing a wise thing and setting a good example. All of God's people need to surrender their bodies to the Lord (Rom. 12:1), and this includes the lips and the tongue. We must also yield our hearts to the Lord, because what comes out of the mouth originates in the heart.

Proverbs 16:1 has been a great help to me, especially when I've been called upon to give counsel: "To man belong the plans of the hearts, but from the Lord comes the reply of the tongue" (NIV). When you couple this with 19:21, it gives you great encouragement: "Many are the plans in a man's heart, but it is the Lord's purpose that prevails" (NIV). On many occasions, I've had to make decisions about complex matters, and the Lord has given me just the words to speak. However, if my heart had not been in touch with His Word and yielded to His will, the Spirit might not have been able to direct me. If we make our plans the best we can and commit them to the Lord, He'll guide us in what we say and do.

God also gives us "spiritual radar" so that we can assess a situation and make the right reply. "The lips of the righteous know what is acceptable" (10:32). "A man has joy by the answer of his mouth, and a word spoken in due season, how good it is" (15:23, NKJV; see Isa. 50:4-6). "The heart of the righteous studies how to answer, but the mouth of the wicked pours forth evil" (Prov. 15:28, NKJV). There is beauty and value in the "word fitly spoken" (25:11-12).

People who speak wisely, saying the right thing at the right time in the right way, are people who store God's truth in their hearts. "Wisdom is found on the lips of him who has understanding" (10:13, NKJV), and that understanding comes from the Word of God. "Wise people store up knowledge" (10:14, NKJV); they are "filled richly" with the Word of God (Col. 3:16). "The heart of the wise teaches his mouth, and adds learning to his lips" (Prov. 16:23, NKJV). If we devote our hearts to serious study of the Word, even while we're sharing the truth with others, God will teach us more of His truth. I have had this happen while ministering the Word, and it's a wonderful experience of God's goodness.

One of my high school teachers used to say, "Empty barrels make the most noise," and she was right. Too often in church board meetings and business meetings, those who talk the most have the least to say. People who don't prepare their hearts for such meetings are making themselves available to become the devil's tools for hindering God's work. If we're filled with the Word and led by the Spirit, we'll be a part of the answer and not a part of the problem.

Have you heard the fable of the king and the menu? A king once asked his cook to prepare for him the best dish in the world, and he was served a dish of tongue. The king then asked for the worst dish in the world, and again was served tongue.

"Why do you serve me the same food as both the best and the worst?" the perplexed monarch asked.

"Because, your majesty," the cook replied, "the tongue is the best of things when used wisely and lovingly, but it is the worst of things when used carelessly and unkindly."

"Death and life are in the power of the tongue" (18:21, NKJV).

"The mouth of the righteous is a fountain of life" (10:11, NIV).

Choose life!

TEN

Make Way for the Righteous!

Those who obey the wisdom taught in God's Word will become more skillful in handling the affairs of life. But we must not think that this wisdom is a set of rules or a collection of "success formulas" that anyone can occasionally apply as he or she pleases. Following God's wisdom is a full-time endeavor. *His Word must first work within our hearts and transform our character before we can become the kind of people God can guide and bless.* You don't need godly character these days to be a success in making money. Many Hollywood celebrities, dishonest businessmen, and deceptive politicians have proved that. But if you're concerned with making a *life,* you must major on building godly character.

This explains why the words *righteous* and *righteousness* are used so often in Proverbs. Wisdom leads, "in the way of righteousness" (8:20) and, "in the way of righteousness is life" (12:28). "The prospect of the righteous is joy, but the hopes of the wicked come to nothing" (10:28, NIV). The wicked have hopes, but they're false hopes, so it behooves us to examine our own hearts to make sure we're among the righteous who truly have hope, and that we're the kind of people the Lord can trust with His blessings.

1. The God of righteousness

The Hebrew words in Proverbs that are translated "righteous," "righteousness," "upright," and "uprightness" describe ethical conduct that conforms to God's standards and moral character that comes from a right relationship to the Lord and His Word. True righteousness isn't just toeing the line and obeying the rules. As Jesus teaches in the Sermon on the Mount, it is possible for us to obey the law outwardly while cultivating sin inwardly. It isn't enough for us not to kill or not to commit adultery; we must also not harbor hatred and lust in our hearts (Matt. 5:21-48).

Our God is a righteous God. His character is holy and without sin (1 John 1:5), and all that He says and does is right and just. "He is the Rock, His work is perfect; for all His ways are justice, a God of truth and without injustice; righteous and upright is He" (Deut. 32:4, NKJV). "For the Lord is righteous, He loves righteousness; His countenance beholds the upright" (Ps. 11:7, NKJV).

God's Word is righteous. "I open my lips to speak what is right. . . . All the words of my mouth are just; none of them is crooked or perverse. To the discerning all of them are right; they are faultless to those who have knowledge" (Prov. 8:6, 8-9, NIV; see Ps. 119:138). The Word of God reveals the God of the Word; His Word, like His character, can be trusted.

Other nations had their gods, temples, priests, and sacrifices, but only the people of Israel worshiped the living God *who spoke to them and gave them His Word.* "Did any people ever hear the voice of God speaking out of the midst of the fire, as you have heard, and live? . . . Out of heaven He let you hear His voice, that He might instruct you; on earth He showed you His great fire, and you heard His words out of the midst of the fire" (Deut. 4:33, 36, NKJV).

However, the privilege of *hearing* God's Word brings with it the responsibility of *obeying* what He commands. "You shall

125

therefore keep His statutes and His commandments which I command you today, that it may go well with you and with your children after you, and that you may prolong your days in the land which the Lord your God is giving you for all time" (Deut. 4:40, NKJV). "See that you do not refuse Him who speaks" (Heb. 12:25, NKJV).

God's acts are righteous. "I am the Lord, who exercises kindness, justice and righteousness on earth, for in these I delight" (Jer. 9:24, NIV). "The Lord our God is righteous in everything He does" (Dan. 9:14, NIV). We may question God's plans and even accuse Him of being unfair, but nobody can succeed in proving that God has ever done anything wrong. "The Lord is righteous in her midst, He will do no unrighteousness. Every morning He brings His justice to light; He never fails" (Zeph. 3:5, NKJV).

God wants His people to be righteous. It is unthinkable that a righteous God would violate His own nature and disobey His own Word by asking His people to be less than righteous. Before He gave Israel His Law, God said: "Now therefore, if you will indeed obey My voice and keep My covenant, then you shall be a special treasure to Me above all people. . . . and you shall be to Me a kingdom of priests and a holy nation" (Ex. 19:5-6, NKJV). Jesus echoed this divine desire when He said, "Therefore you shall be perfect, just as your Father in heaven is perfect" (Matt. 5:48, NKJV).

The problem, of course, is that people are—people. And that means that they're sinners. "Every way of a man is right in his own eyes, but the Lord weighs the hearts" (Prov. 21:2, NKJV). "There is not a righteous man on earth who does what is right and never sins" (Ecc. 7:20, NIV). "There is none righteous, no, not one" (Rom. 3:10; see Ps. 14:1-3). How can sinners ever be righteous before a righteous God?

When you read Proverbs, you discover that God mentions many different sins that people committed in ancient Israel and still commit in our communities today, sins like anger, deception, thievery, murder, slander, gossip, drunkenness, adultery, bribery, jealousy, rebellion against parents, and a host of other things that all of us would recognize. Proverbs makes it very clear that people are sinners.

God provides righteousness for those who will accept it. How can a guilty sinner ever become righteous enough to please a holy God? If God is going to be just, all He can do is condemn the wicked and accept the righteous, but there are no righteous people for Him to accept! We certainly don't become righteous by being religious. "To do righteousness and justice is more acceptable to the Lord than sacrifice" (Prov. 21:3). Disobedient King Saul learned that lesson from Samuel (1 Sam. 15:22), and this important principle was repeated by several other prophets (Isa. 1:11-17; Jer. 7:22-23; Micah 6:6-8). In fact, Isaiah said that our righteousnesses were "as filthy rags" in God's sight (Isa. 64:6) — so what must our *sins* look like to Him?

"He who justifies the wicked, and he who condemns the just, both of them alike are an abomination to the Lord" (Prov. 17:15, NKJV). *But that's exactly what the Lord God did!* His Son, Jesus Christ, died for the sins of the world, "the just for the unjust" (1 Peter 3:18); the judgment that should have been ours was laid on Him (2:24). God justifies (declares righteous) the ungodly, not when they do good works but when they put their faith in Christ. "But to him who does not work [for righteousness] but believes on Him who justifies the ungodly, his faith is accounted for righteousness" (Rom. 4:5, NKJV).[1]

"The wicked shall be a ransom for the righteous," wrote Solomon, "and the transgressor for the upright" (Prov. 21:18), but that wasn't true at Calvary. There the Righteous One became a ransom for the wicked when Jesus was numbered with the transgressors and died for our sins (Isa. 53:4-

6, 12). The only way to be righteous before God is to trust Jesus Christ and receive His righteousness as God's free gift (Rom. 5:17; 2 Cor. 5:21).[2] Then we can begin to walk "the path of righteousness" and enjoy the blessings of the Lord.

Not everybody who claims to be among the righteous is truly a child of God. God's people *understand righteousness* (Prov. 2:9) because they meditate on His Word and seek to obey it. They *do righteousness* (1:3; 25:26) because true faith always leads to works (James 2:14-26). They *speak righteousness* (Prov. 10:11; 12:6, 17; 13:5; 15:28; 16:13) and their words can be trusted, and they *pursue righteousness* and make it the passion of their hearts. "The Lord detests the way of the wicked, but He loves those who pursue righteousness" (15:9, NIV). "Blessed are they who hunger and thirst for righteousness; for they shall be filled" (Matt. 5:6).

When people are right with God, He leads them in "right paths" (Prov. 4:11), and teaches them "right things" (8:6). Their minds and hearts are filled with right thoughts (12:5), and their lips speak right words (23:16). Their work is right (21:8), because God works in them and through them to accomplish His will (Phil. 2:12-13).

2. The path of righteousness
In our study of Proverbs 2–4, we learned that following the way of wisdom is compared to a pilgrim walking a path. As we follow His wisdom, God protects, directs, and perfects our path. God's desire for us is that we "walk in the way of goodness, and keep to the paths of righteousness" (2:20). We're warned not to listen to evil men "who leave the paths of uprightness to walk in the ways of darkness" (v. 13, NKJV); nor should we heed the seductive words of the evil woman whose "house leads down to death, and her paths to the dead" (v. 18, NKJV).

I read about a dirt-road intersection in the prairies of Canada where somebody had posted this sign: "Be careful what rut you take—you'll be on it a long time!" Each of us must choose to travel one of two paths, and the path we choose determines the destination we'll reach (Matt. 7:13-14). It also determines the quality of life we'll experience along the way. Solomon points out some of the blessings that come to those who walk the path of life and wisdom.

To begin with, God's people experience His *direction*. "The righteousness of the blameless will direct his way aright, but the wicked will fall by his own wickedness" (Prov. 11:5, NKJV). The Lord directs the paths of those who trust and obey (3:5-6), because God wants His children to know His will (Acts 22:14) and enjoy doing it (Eph. 6:6). The Lord reveals His will only to those who are willing to obey it (John 7:17).

On the path of the righteous, God's people also experience *deliverance*. "The righteousness of the upright shall deliver them, but transgressors shall be taken in their own naughtiness" (Prov. 11:6). Godly people certainly have their share of trials and testings, but the Lord promises to help them and make these experiences turn out for good (Rom. 8:28). "The righteous cry out, and the Lord hears, and delivers them out of all their troubles" (Ps. 34:17). Obedience to the Lord keeps us from many of the troubles that sinners experience, but when the Lord permits us to suffer, He promises to bring us through. "The wicked is snared by the transgression of his lips, but the just shall come out of trouble" (Prov. 12:13).

We have God's *provision* for all we need if we're walking in His wisdom. "I walk in the way of righteousness, along the paths of justice, bestowing wealth on those who love me and making their treasuries full" (8:20-21, NIV). This isn't an encouragement for us to jump on the "health-wealth-and-success" bandwagon. Proverbs was originally written for Jews under the Old Covenant; under that covenant, material blessing was a part of God's promise to Israel (Deut. 28:1-14).

Believers today can be sure of God's provision for their every need as they obey His will (Phil. 4:19; Matt. 6:24-34).

It sometimes looks to us as though the righteous are suffering and the wicked prospering, but faith sees beyond today and considers where the godless end up (Ps. 73). "Better is a little with righteousness than great revenues without right [with injustice]" (Prov. 16:8). Our real prosperity isn't here on earth but in glory when we see the Lord. "Misfortune pursues the sinners, but prosperity is the reward of the righteous" (13:21, NIV).

3. The influence of righteousness

The life of righteousness must not become a solitary and selfish experience. *When God blesses the righteous, He does it so they can share the blessing with others.* "I will bless you," God promised Abraham, "and you shall be a blessing" (Gen. 12:2, NKJV). The "blessed man" of Psalm 1 is "like a tree" that produces fruit for *others* to enjoy (Ps. 1:3). "The righteous will thrive like a green leaf.... The fruit of the righteous is a tree of life" (Prov. 11:28, 30, NIV).

Let's trace the circles of influence that radiate from the lives of men and women of God who walk on His paths.

They are blessed in their character. The eminent American preacher Phillips Brooks said that the purpose of life was the building of character through truth. Christian character is one thing we'll take to heaven with us. We'll all have glorified bodies like that of our Lord (Phil. 3:20-21; 1 John 3:1-3), and we'll all be happy in His presence, but we will not all immediately have the same capacity for appreciating spiritual things. Every vessel will be filled, but not all vessels will be the same size. Those who have walked closely with their Lord will be delighted to see Him (2 Tim. 4:8), but others will be "ashamed before Him at His coming" (1 John 2:28).

The righteous desire the very best from the Lord, and He

grants it to them (Prov. 10:24; 11:23). When we delight ourselves in the Lord, we will want the things that delight Him
(Ps. 37:4). The developing of spiritual perception, a godly
appetite, and the ability to choose the best (Phil. 1:9-11), is
one of the blessed by-products of a holy walk with God. The
more we become like Christ, the less we enjoy the "entertainment" of this world and long for the enrichment of the
world to come.

Of course, godly character comes from feeding on the
Word and taking time to be holy. "Give instruction to a wise
man, and he will be yet wiser; teach a just man, and he will
increase in learning" (Prov. 9:9). Even reproof helps the godly person to mature. "Do not correct a scoffer, lest he hate
you; rebuke a wise man, and he will love you" (v. 8, NKJV).

The righteous are kind and generous (21:26) and show
their kindness, not only in the way they treat people (29:7)
but also in the way they treat animals. "A righteous man
regards the life of his animal, but the tender mercies of the
wicked are cruel" (12:10, NKJV).

They are blessed in their home. "The Lord's curse is on the
house of the wicked, but He blesses the home of the righteous" (3:33, NIV). "The house of the wicked will be overthrown, but the tent of the upright will flourish" (14:11,
NKJV). The wicked may live in houses, and the righteous have
only tents, but with the blessing of the Lord, the righteous
person's tent will be a palace! "The wicked are overthrown,
and are not: but the house of the righteous shall stand"
(12:7).

In the Hebrew culture, "house" refers to the family as well
as the structure in which the family dwells (2 Sam. 7:16, 25,
27), which means that the children of the godly are included
in the blessing. "The righteous man walks in his integrity;
his children are blessed after him" (20:7, NKJV). "Through
wisdom a house is built, and by understanding it is estab-

lished; by knowledge the rooms are filled with all precious and pleasant riches" (24:3-4; see 14:1).

One of the greatest rewards in life is to be a blessing to your children and grandchildren. "I have been young, and now am old; yet I have not seen the righteous forsaken, nor his descendants begging bread" (Ps. 37:25, NKJV). This blessing includes material things (Prov. 13:22), but it applies even more to spiritual treasures.

When I was born, a doctor told my parents that I wouldn't live beyond the age of two; yet the Lord enabled them to raise me, even though I wasn't a robust child. Why did I survive? Partly because of a great grandfather who had prayed years before that there would be a preacher of the Gospel in every generation of our family—and there has been! "The memory of the just is blessed: but the name of the wicked shall rot" (10:7).

"Like a bird that strays from its nest is a man who strays from his home" (27:8, NIV). In our contemporary American society, about 17 percent of the population relocates each year, but in ancient Israel, people stayed close to home. The extended family was the norm, with children and grandchildren learning to revere their ancestors and respectfully learning from them. The person who strayed from home was either up to no good or had to leave because of family problems.

But the verse applies spiritually as well as geographically: We must not stray from the example of our godly ancestors or the spiritual treasures they left us. How tragic it is when children and grandchildren ridicule and reject the spiritual heritage of their family and turn instead to the ways of the world.

They are blessed as citizens and leaders. "When it goes well with the righteous, the city rejoices; and when the wicked perish, there is jubilation. By the blessing of the upright the city is exalted, but it is overthrown by the mouth of the wicked" (11:10-11, NKJV). "When the righteous are in authority, the people rejoice; but when a wicked man rules, the people groan" (29:2, NKJV).

Israel was a monarchy and the king was expected to rule in the fear of the Lord (20:8, 26). "It is an abomination to kings to commit wickedness: for the throne is established by righteousness" (16:12). "Take away the wicked from before the king, and his throne shall be established in righteousness" (25:5). God cast out the Canaanite nations because their sins were abominable to Him (Deut. 12:29-32), and He chastened Israel when they imitated the sins of those nations (Jud. 2). God would not tolerate the sin of idolatry.

By turning away from God's Law, wicked rulers led the way for the nation to become evil. Whenever the nation had a godly king, such as David, Josiah, or Hezekiah, God blessed His people. But when an ungodly king ascended the throne, the Lord withdrew His blessing and left them to their own devices. Eventually, the Northern Kingdom of Israel was taken over by Assyria, the Southern Kingdom of Judah was exiled in Babylon, and Jerusalem and the temple destroyed.

During times of spiritual decay, it was the godly remnant of righteous people who maintained the flickering flame of spiritual life in the nation. When false prophets, greedy priests, and ruthless kings joined together to lead the nation away from the true God, it was the faithful remnant that served as salt and light in the land. "Then they that feared the Lord spake often one to another: and the Lord hearkened, and heard it, and a book of remembrance was written before Him for them that feared the Lord, and that thought upon His name" (Mal. 3:16).

Israel is the only nation that has a special covenant relationship with God, but the principle of Proverbs 14:34 still stands: "Righteousness exalts a nation, but sin is a disgrace to any people" (NIV). Deuteronomy 12, Amos 1–2, and Romans 1:18-32 make it clear that God judges the Gentile nations for their sins even though He didn't give them the same law that He gave to Israel (Ps. 147:19-20). National leaders can't escape the judgment of God when they lead the people away from God's holy standards. Legalizing sin doesn't make it right. No wonder Thomas Jefferson wrote, "Indeed I tremble for my country when I reflect that God is just."

Godly parents can raise godly children, and godly children can provide godly influence in their communities and in the nation. In a democracy, where leadership is elected and not inherited, the Lord's remnant must exert as much influence for righteousness as possible; certainly every believer ought to pray for those in authority (1 Tim. 2:1-8). I have ministered the Word in hundreds of churches and conferences in the United States, and I confess that rarely have I heard government leaders mentioned in the pulpit prayers. If the church obeyed the Word and prayed, national leaders would have to take God into account in their deliberations. "The king's heart is in the hand of the Lord; He directs it like a watercourse wherever He pleases" (Prov. 21:1, NIV).

I occasionally hear people lamenting the state of the nation, but most of them fail to point out the main cause: *The church collectively and believers individually aren't doing their job in spreading righteousness.* If the righteous remnant were spreading more salt and light, there would be less decay and darkness (Matt. 5:13-16). Christians have a job to do: praying for all in authority, winning the lost, living godly lives, and raising godly children.

And it would help if we humbled ourselves and sought God's face (2 Chron. 7:14); for apart from the deep working of God's Spirit in hearts, there is no hope for any nation.

"Blessed is the nation whose God is the Lord, the people He chose for His inheritance" (Ps. 33:12, NIV).

ELEVEN

Enjoying God's Guidance

Mention the phrase, "the will of God," and you'll get different responses from different people, not all of them positive.

Some people will say, "Not that again!" They remember their adolescent years when it seemed like every lesson and sermon they heard hammered away on knowing and doing God's will, and it all seemed so impractical to them at that time.

Others will smile knowingly, recalling the difficult "valley experiences" of life when the only thing that kept them going was depending on the will of God. The will of God wasn't always easy, but it was always good and right.

Perhaps some people will say nothing, but they'll feel a hidden inward pain as they remember how they deliberately disobeyed God's will and suffered for it. They had to learn the hard way how to delight in the will of God.

No matter how we may feel personally about the topic, if we're going to be skillful in life, we have to understand what God's will is and how it works in our everyday experience. In the Book of Proverbs, Solomon shares with us the essentials for knowing, doing, and enjoying the will of God.

1. Faith

"Trust in the Lord with all your heart, and lean not on your own understanding; in all your ways acknowledge Him, and He shall direct your paths" (Prov. 3:5-6, NKJV). These two verses have encouraged believers everywhere in their quest for God's guidance, and for those who have sincerely met the conditions, the promise has never failed. But when we say, "I'm trusting in the Lord," what are we really affirming?

That we belong to God. No unbeliever could honestly rest on the words of Proverbs 3:5-6. While a sovereign God can rule and overrule in the life of any person, saved or lost,[1] it is clear that the life of the unsaved person is motivated and energized by the world, the flesh, and the devil (Eph. 2:1-3). Only a believer can have the guidance of the indwelling Holy Spirit or understand the teachings of the Scriptures, and only a believer would really *want* to understand and obey the will of God.

That God has a plan for our lives. "Many are the plans in a man's heart, but it is the Lord's purpose that prevails" (Prov. 19:21, NIV). It is inconceivable that our loving Heavenly Father would give His Son to die for us, and then abandon us to our own ways! We are not our own because we have been purchased by God (1 Cor. 6:19-20), so it's reasonable that our Master should have a perfect plan for us to fulfill for His glory. Ephesians 2:10 assures us that the good works God wants us to accomplish have already been determined; in Philippians 2:12-13, God assures us that He works in us to accomplish His good pleasure. The talents we were born with (Ps. 139:13-18) and the gifts we received at conversion (1 Cor. 12:1-11) are brought together by the Holy Spirit so that we can do what God has called us to do.

That this plan is the best thing for us. How could a holy God will for His children anything less than His best, and how could a loving God plan anything that would harm us? We have no reason to fear the will of God, because His plans come from His heart. "The counsel of the Lord stands forever, the plans of His heart to all generations" (Ps. 33:11, NKJV). Unless we see the will of God as the expression of the love of God, we'll resist it stubbornly, or do it grudgingly, instead of enjoying it. Faith in God's love and wisdom will transform our attitude and make the will of God nourishment instead of punishment (John 4:34).

That the Father will reveal His will in His time. It's through "faith and patience" that we receive what God promises (Heb. 6:12, 15), and it's as dangerous to run ahead of the Lord as it is to stubbornly lag behind. "It is not good to have zeal without knowledge, nor to be hasty and miss the way" (Prov. 19:2, NIV). "Be not like the horse or like the mule" (Ps. 32:9). The horse rushes ahead and the mule won't budge, and both attitudes are wrong. Even the great Apostle Paul didn't always know exactly the way God was guiding, and he had to pause in his work and wait for divine direction (Acts 16:6-10). Our times are in His hand (Ps. 31:15), and the Father is always on schedule (John 11:6-10).

2. Commitment

Knowing and obeying the will of God can't be a halfhearted endeavor on our part, a hobby we indulge in when there's an emergency or when we "feel like it." God wants us to trust Him with *all* our heart and acknowledge Him in *all* our ways. Knowing and doing the will of God isn't a "spiritual technique" that we use occasionally; it's a committed lifestyle that involves everything we do.

Successful athletes make winning their full-time pursuit, and this shows up in the way they eat, sleep, exercise, and relate to their coaches and teammates. The word for this is commitment, and commitment involves obedience. "He who scorns instruction will pay for it, but he who respects a command is rewarded" (Prov. 13:13, NIV).

In the Book of Proverbs, the wise father repeatedly gives his son loving calls to obedience. "My son, do not forget my law, but let your heart keep my commands" (3:1, NKJV). "My son, keep your father's command, and do not forsake the law of your mother" (6:20, NKJV). "My son, keep my words, and treasure my commands within you" (7:1, NKJV). *The will of God isn't a curiosity for us to study, it's a command for us to obey; God isn't obligated to reveal His will unless we're willing to do it.* "If anyone wants to do His will, he shall know concerning the doctrine, whether it is from God or whether I speak on My own authority" (John 7:17, NKJV). As F.W. Robertson said, "Obedience is the organ of spiritual knowledge."

This commitment is spelled out in Romans 12:1-2, another familiar passage about the will of God. Before I can "prove by experience" what God's will is, and discover that His will is "good, pleasing and perfect" (NIV), I must give Him my body, my mind, and my will, a total commitment of my total being. This is a once-for-all presentation, but it needs to be renewed daily as we meet with the Lord in worship and prayer.

A pastor friend of mine once said to me, "There are too many 'cafeteria Christians' in our congregation. Instead of letting God plan the whole meal and accepting it, they pick and choose what they want, and they miss the best dishes He fixes for them!" God wants all of our heart, and He expects us to obey all of His will in all of our ways. If Jesus Christ gave His all for us, how can we do less than give our all to Him?

The Hebrew word translated "acknowledge" in Proverbs 3:6 carries with it the idea of intimate communion and is used to describe the marriage relationship (Gen. 4:l; 19:8). Whenever I find myself distant from my Father, then I know that I've allowed something to enter my life that is not in the sphere of His will. Since the will of God comes from the heart of God, it ought to draw my heart closer to Him.

3. Instruction

"A wise son heeds his father's instruction" (Prov. 13:1, NIV). "Take firm hold of instruction, do not let go; keep her, for she is your life" (4:13, NKJV). "Give instruction to a wise man, and he will be yet wiser: teach a just man, and he will increase in learning" (9:9).

In order to "trust in the Lord," we must have His Word to instruct us, because "faith comes by hearing, and hearing by the word of God" (Rom. 10:17, NKJV). Scripture is "the word of faith" (Rom. 10:8) which generates and nourishes faith in our hearts, and we can depend on His Word. "Every word of God is pure; He is a shield to those who put their trust in Him" (Prov. 30:5, NKJV; see 22:17-21).

To deliberately act apart from the instruction of the Scriptures is to rebel against the revealed will of God. "He who despises the word will be destroyed, but he who fears the commandment will be rewarded" (13:13, NKJV; see 19:16). To ignore the Word of God is to deprive ourselves of the guidance we need for making the decisions of life. "Stop listening to instruction, my son, and you will stray from the words of knowledge" (19:27, NIV).

Most of the situations, opportunities, and decisions the average person encounters in life are already dealt with in the Word of God. Consult a topical index to the Bible, or even to the Book of Proverbs, and you'll see how thoroughly Scripture deals with the practical affairs of life. Of course, we can't expect the Bible to specifically tell us the name of the person we should marry, which job we should accept, what car we should buy, or where to spend our vacation, but if we're saturated with God's wisdom and sincerely seeking His will, we'll be ready for Him to guide us by His Spirit and the providential circumstances of life.

"A man's steps are of the Lord; how then can a man understand his own way?" (20:24, NKJV) God overruled Joseph's brothers' envy and used their evil deeds to build Joseph's faith and save Jacob's family (Gen. 50:20). At the time, nobody could understand what the Lord was doing, but He was working out His perfect plan. In the school of faith, sometimes we don't know what the lesson was until we've passed — or failed — the examination!

When we studied Proverbs 1–4, we learned that it is necessary for us to *apply ourselves* to God's Word if we hope to receive His instruction. According to Proverbs 2:1-4, our responsibility is to receive the Word, treasure it, listen to it, apply our heart to it, cry out for it, and search for it the way a miner searches for treasure; *then* we will "understand the fear of the Lord, and find the knowledge of God" (2:5, NKJV).

Reading and meditating on God's Word ought to be a daily habit with us. "Blessed is the man who listens to me," says Wisdom, "watching daily at my gates, waiting at the posts of my doors" (8:34, NKJV). If you want your faith and spiritual discernment to mature, there's no substitute for the disciplined, systematic reading of the whole Word of God. "Wise people store up knowledge" (10:14, NKJV), because you never know when you'll need some truth from the Bible to help you overcome a temptation or make a decision.

But there's another factor involved, and that's *prayer*, because the Word of God and prayer go together (John 15:7; Acts 6:4; Eph. 6:17-18). "If anyone turns a deaf ear to the law, even his prayers are detestable" (Prov. 28:9, NIV; see 15:8). The word translated "law" in this verse is *torah,* which means "instruction." If I won't listen to God's instruction, why should God listen to my petition?

4. Counsel

"Plans are established by counsel; by wise counsel wage war" (20:18, NKJV). If experienced generals seek counsel as they wage war, shouldn't we seek counsel for the battles of life? It's dangerous to rely on our own wisdom and experience and to ignore the wisdom and experience of other believers who have successfully walked with the Lord. "The way of a fool is right in his own eyes, but he who heeds counsel is wise" (12:15, NKJV).

The first source of wise counsel is *Christian parents.* "Listen to your father who begot you, and do not despise your mother when she is old" (23:22, NKJV; see 6:20-23). "A wise son heeds his father's instruction" (13:1, NKJV). Not everybody has the privilege of being raised in a godly home, but even then, the Lord often provides "substitute parents" who can share the wisdom of the Lord.

Christian friends can also listen, counsel, and pray. "Ointment and perfume delight the heart, and the sweetness of a man's friend gives delight by hearty counsel" (27:9, NKJV). *The Living Bible* paraphrases the verse, "Friendly suggestions are as pleasant as perfume," but sometimes a friend's counsel may not be perfume! It may be acid! Even then, we have nothing to lose; for "as iron sharpens iron, so a man sharpens the countenance of his friend" (27:17, NKJV). The sparks may fly, but God will give us the light that we need. "Faithful are the wounds of a friend, but the kisses of an enemy are deceitful" (27:6).

How we accept and apply rebuke is a test of how devoted we are to truth and wisdom and how sincere we are in wanting to know God's will. "He who listens to a life-giving rebuke will be at home among the wise" (15:31, NIV). "He who disdains instruction despises his own soul, but he who heeds rebuke gets understanding" (v. 32, NKJV). Friends who flatter us and avoid telling us the truth are only doing us harm. "He who rebukes a man will in the end gain more favor than he who has a flattering tongue" (28:23, NIV; see 29:5).

Not every friend is a good counselor, so we must choose wisely. "The purposes of a man's heart are deep waters, but a man of understanding draws them out" (20:5, NIV). We don't know our own hearts (Jer. 17:9), and only God's Word can honestly reveal "the thoughts and intents [motives] of the heart" (Heb. 4:12). It takes a counselor with loving patience and a discerning spirit to help us see what lies deep within our hearts.

While it's usually true that "a multitude of counselors" assures a wise decision (Prov. 11:14; 15:22; 24:6; see Ex. 23:2), at the same time, we must avoid running from friend to friend asking for advice. This may indicate that we're trying to find somebody who will tell us what we want to hear! "A man of many companions may come to ruin, but there is a friend who sticks closer than a brother" (Prov. 18:24, NIV).[2] It isn't enough to have friends; we must have *a friend* who will "speak the truth in love" (Eph. 4:15).

Often in my conference ministry, people will approach me with personal problems and ask for advice. I try to avoid giving counsel for several reasons: I don't know the people; I'm not going to be there long enough to continue a counseling relationship; a quick chat after a meeting isn't counseling; and I don't want to take the place of a faithful local pastor.

"Have you discussed this matter with your pastor?" I ask, and I carefully listen to the reply. No matter what the words are, the reply often indicates, "I talked to him, but it didn't do any good" (meaning possibly, "I didn't get my way") or, "I've talked to him and a dozen other ministers and guest speakers!" Then I know that anything I say will probably do little good.

In seeking counsel, we must be sincere, because a loving and wise friend can often see dangers and detours that are hidden from us. It's best to be accountable to another believer and submit to the authority of the spiritual leaders in our church. During more than forty years of ministry, I've witnessed the painful downfalls of several "Lone Ranger" Christians who thought they didn't need anybody's counsel. "A man who isolates himself seeks his own desire; he rages against all wise judgment" (Prov. 18:1, NKJV). Christians are God's sheep, and we need to flock together. As members of Christ's spiritual body (1 Cor. 12), we belong to each other and we need each other.

5. Plans

We must never think that in determining the will of God, the believer is passive and only the Lord is active. "Let go and let God" is a clever motto, but I'm not sure it applies to every area of the Christian life.[3] If all we do is exercise faith, commit our way to the Lord, read the Bible, and counsel with our friends, we may never get much done for the Lord. You can't steer a car when it's in neutral, and "faith without works is dead" (James 2:26).

But doesn't Proverbs 3:5 warn us against leaning on our own understanding? Yes, it does, but the word "leaning" means "to rely on," and our faith must be in God's Word and not in our own wisdom. It's the same word used of a king who leans on the arm of an officer (2 Kings 5:18; 7:2, 17) or a person who leans on a staff (18:21).

As we seek to know God's will, we must gather all the facts we can and assess them, because our decision must be based on knowledge and not hearsay. "Every prudent man acts out of knowledge, but a fool exposes his folly" (Prov. 13:16, NIV). "He who answers a matter before he hears it, it is folly and shame to him" (18:13, NKJV). This applies whether we're answering somebody else or answering the Lord. "The wisdom of the prudent is to give thought to their ways, but the folly of fools is deception" (14:8, NIV). We must take time for an honest look at facts.

God expects us to use our brains and make plans, but He also expects us to submit those plans to Him and let Him make the final decision. "To man belong the plans of the heart, but from the Lord comes the reply of the tongue" (16:1, NIV). "Commit to the Lord whatever you do, and your plans will succeed" (v. 3, NIV). If we're yielded to the Lord and our plans are not His plans, He will show us what's right and steer us away from what's wrong. "And if on some point you think differently, that too God will make clear to you" (Phil. 3:15, NIV). "In his heart a man plans his course, but the Lord determines his steps" (Prov. 16:9, NIV).

It is when we rebel against the Lord and want to go our own way that we get into trouble. "There is no wisdom nor understanding nor counsel against the Lord" (21:30). That's why we must begin our search for God's will by reading His Word and obeying it, because the Scriptures reveal the character and the purposes of God. The will of God will never contradict either the purposes of God or the character of God, so we must wait before the Lord, because "the plans of the diligent lead to profit as surely as haste leads to poverty" (21:5, NIV). If we're walking by faith, we won't rush ahead, for, "whoever believes will not act hastily" (Isa. 28:16, NKJV).

So, when we have a decision to make, we gather all the facts and seek wise counsel, we make our plans, we commit ourselves and our plans to the Lord, we listen to His Word, and we wait before Him for His leading. Sometimes God leads us through a Bible promise or warning; sometimes while we're at worship with God's people, He speaks through a song or Scripture reading; or He may direct us through providential circumstances. More than once in my own life, His disciplines have turned out to be His directions (Prov. 3:11-12; Heb. 12:1-11).

6. Obedience

"In all your ways acknowledge Him" (Prov. 3:6) means, "Do God's will in every area of life. Seek to honor Him in everything." Note verse 7, "Do not be wise in your own eyes; fear the Lord and depart from evil" (NKJV). Pride and disobedience in any area of life can get us on dangerous detours, so we must stay humble before Him. "When pride comes, then comes shame; but with the humble is wisdom. The integrity of the upright will guide them, but the perversity of the unfaithful will destroy them" (11:2-3, NKJV).

The assurance is, "and He shall direct your paths." Dr. G. Campbell Morgan said: "Not always in easy or pleasant paths, but always in right paths. Not always in those I would have chosen, but always in paths which lead to success. . . . The paths that He directs lead always through mist and mystery, through battle and through bruising, to the fulfillment of the meaning of life."[4]

Some people live only for entertainment and try to escape the burdens of life. Others live for enjoyment and try to make the most of life. God's dedicated people live for enrichment and discover fulfillment in life as they do the will of God from the heart.

Which one are you?

TWELVE

Popular Sins (Drunkenness, Disrespect, Illusion, Greed, Pride)

Thanks to worldwide media coverage and the constant pressure for higher program ratings, sin has become an important part of international entertainment. Evil activities that we ought to be weeping over are now sources of entertainment; they are vividly displayed on movie and TV screens and discussed in depth in newspapers and magazines. The all-seeing camera moves into the bedroom, the barroom, and the courtroom and enables excited viewers to enjoy sin vicariously. Movies and TV are instructing generation after generation of children how to ridicule virginity, laugh at sobriety, challenge authority, and reject honesty. Actors, actresses, and advertisers have convinced them that "having fun," "feeling good," and "getting away with it" are now the main goals in life.

The Book of Proverbs has something to say about popular sins that are weakening our homes, threatening the peace of our communities, and destroying lives.

1. Drunkenness
Alcohol is a narcotic, not a food; Proverbs warns us about alcohol abuse. We need to heed that warning today. Paying

for the tragic consequences of drug and alcohol abuse in the United States drains $200 billion annually out of the economy, which averages out to approximately $800 per citizen per year. About 50,000 people a year are killed by drunk drivers, and millions of work hours are lost because of alcohol related absences and work accidents. The United States consumes 60 percent of the world's illicit drugs (alcohol is a legal drug), and drug users spend $150 billion in the United States just on cocaine![1]

Wine and Israel. Wine is mentioned nearly 150 times in the Old Testament. The people of Israel considered it a gift from God, along with oil and bread (Ps. 104:15). When Isaac blessed Jacob, he asked God to give him "the dew of heaven, and the fatness of the earth, and plenty of corn [grain] and wine" (Gen. 27:28; see also Deut. 7:13). However, milk and water, not wine, were the usual daily drinks at Jewish tables; like meat, wine was usually kept for special festive occasions. The Jews also had "strong drink," which was brewed from fermented grain or fruit.

While drunkenness is condemned by the Law and the Prophets,[2] the use of wine was not forbidden, except to priests serving in the holy precincts (Lev. 10:8-10) and to people under a Nazirite vow (Num. 6:1-12). Wine was used as a drink offering to the Lord (Ex. 29:38-41; Num. 15:1-15), and could be brought as part of the Jews' tithes (Neh. 10:36-39), so wine itself wasn't considered sinful. The problem was what wine *dia* to people. The Old Testament doesn't demand total abstinence, although certainly it recommends it.[3]

Wine and wisdom. "Wine is a mocker, intoxicating drink arouses brawling, and whoever is led astray by it is not wise" (Prov. 20:1, NKJV). This is the first of several passages in Proverbs that warn against what today we call "alcohol abuse." Alcohol mocks people by creating in them a thirst for more while not satisfying that thirst. The more people drink, the less they enjoy it. The drinker becomes a drunk and then a brawler. In spite of what the slick advertising says about the charm of drink, it just isn't a smart thing to do. As a Japanese proverb puts it, "First the man takes a drink; then the drink takes a drink; then the drink takes the man."

Alcohol also mocks people by giving them a false sense of happiness and strength, and this is what often leads to fights. The weakling thinks he's a superman so he challenges anybody who gets in his way. The grade-school dropout thinks he's the wisest person in town and argues with anybody who disagrees with him.

As I was writing this chapter, I read an item in the newspaper that illustrates my point. According to the Associated Press, a British charter plane had to make an emergency landing in Munich because a drunken passenger slugged his girlfriend and started brawling with other passengers. German police had to handcuff the man and drag him off the plane. After sobering up in an airport security cell, the man discovered that the airport had charged him $3,000 for the emergency landing and extra jet fuel. Those were expensive drinks![4]

Addiction to alcohol can lead to poverty (21:17), so it's wise to stay away from the people who encourage you to drink (23:20-21). Proverbs 23:29-35 is the most vivid description of the tragic consequences of drunkenness you will find anywhere in Scripture,[5] including delirium, sorrow, strife, bruises, and bloodshot eyes;[6] "and in the end it bites like a snake and poisons like a viper" (23:32, NIV). You'd think that after having this frightening experience, the drinker would want to become a total abstainer for life, but alas, he's a slave! "When will I wake up so I can find another drink?" (v. 35, NIV)

Alcohol and civic responsibilities don't mix, according to Proverbs 31:1-9;[7] yet the alcohol flows freely under capitol domes and at embassies. A resident of Washington, D.C., said to me, "There are three parties in this city: the Republican Party, the Democratic Party, and the cocktail party."

King Lemuel's mother warned him to stay away from wine so that he would be capable of serving others. "Woe to you, O land, when your king is a child, and your princes feast in the morning! Blessed are you, O land, when your king is the son of nobles, and your princes feast at the proper time—for strength and not for drunkenness" (Ecc. 10:16-17, NKJV; see Hosea 7:5). "Woe to those who are heroes at drinking wine and champions at mixing drinks, who acquit the guilty for a bribe, but deny justice to the innocent" (Isa. 5:22, NIV). That's what the queen mother was warning her son to avoid.

Proverbs 31:6-7 seems to suggest that there are times when wine should be used to help people, such as encouraging the dying or comforting the suffering so they can forget their troubles. I think verses 6-7 are spoken in irony and not as a commandment, because nobody's problems are solved by forgetting them, and who wants to spend his or her last minutes of life on earth drunk? When Jesus faced death on the cross, He refused to accept the wine sedative that was offered Him (Matt. 27:33-34). If it's wrong for the king to drink wine because it prevents him from helping people, then it's wrong for needy people to drink wine *because it prevents them from helping themselves!* The dying person needs help in preparing to meet God, and the suffering person needs help in solving life's problems; drinking alcohol will accomplish neither one.[8]

We help people, not by deadening them to their problems and pains, but by encouraging them to trust the Lord and lean on His Word. We certainly must stand up for the oppressed (Prov. 31:8-9) but they also need to be in shape to stand up for themselves, something alcohol won't supply.

Wine and today's believer. The New Testament clearly

warns today's Christians about the sin of drunkenness. "Let us walk properly, as in the day, not in revelry and drunkenness, not in lewdness and lust, not in strife and envy" (Rom. 13:13, NKJV; see 1 Thes. 5:7; Luke 21:34). Galatians 5:21 names drunkenness as one of the works of the flesh, and 1 Peter 2:11 admonishes us to "abstain from fleshly lusts which war against the soul."

Passages like Romans 14:1–15:13 and 1 Corinthians 8–10 instruct us to: (1) receive other Christians and not make differences about diets and special days a test of fellowship or spirituality; (2) avoid being a stumbling block to others; (3) seek to build one another up in Christian maturity; and (4) avoid being obstinate and defensive about our own personal convictions so that they become a cause of disunity in the church. Christians with a weak conscience stumble easily and need to be built up, but stronger Christians are sometimes quick to criticize and look down on others. Both groups need love, patience, and the help of the Spirit.

My wife and I have traveled enough to know that there's such a thing among God's people as "cultural Christianity." Practices that are acceptable in one place may be classified as sins in another place, and this includes the use of alcohol as a beverage. Christians everywhere should deplore drunkenness, but not all of us agree on total abstinence or even on what "moderation" is.

Our conviction is total abstinence, but we haven't made it a test of fellowship or spirituality. As far as I know, we've never created problems ministering in different cultures, even in the homes of people who disagreed with our views. Other Christians have respected us because we've respected them and tried to manifest Christian love. But by not using alcoholic beverages, my wife and I have not been tempted to get drunk; we've also been examples to believers who might stumble if we did drink. These two blessings are worth more to us than whatever pleasure there may be in drinking alcoholic beverages.[9]

2. Disrespect

"The eye that mocks his father, and scorns obedience to his mother, the ravens of the valley will pick it out, and the young eagles will eat it" (Prov. 30:17, NKJV). The child who looks at his or her parents with contempt and disrespect will one day be treated like an unburied corpse, and to be left unburied was a great reproach in Israel. As I read the newspapers and news magazines, I become more and more convinced that we're living in the generation described in Proverbs 30:11-14 with its pride, greed, violence, and lack of appreciation for parents.

Disrespect for parents usually begins with disrespect for the Word of God that parents seek to teach to their children. "A fool despises his father's instruction" (15:5). "He who despises the word will be destroyed, but he who fears the commandment will be rewarded" (13:13). Sometimes children go off to college or university and get poisoned by ideas that are contrary to Scripture, and then they come home to tell everybody how stupid and old-fashioned their parents are. If children maintain this haughty attitude, they'll eventually rob their parents (28:24), curse their parents (20:20), and bring shame to their parents (19:26).

Under the Old Covenant, children who disobeyed their parents and broke the law were in danger of losing their lives. I'm not advocating that disrespect for parents be made a capital crime today, but passages like Deuteronomy 21:18-21 and Leviticus 20:9 show how seriously God takes the Fifth Commandment: "Honor your father and your mother, that your days may be long upon the land which the Lord your God is giving you" (Ex. 20:12, NKJV; see Eph. 6:1-4). Children who don't respect godly, loving parents aren't likely to re-

151

spect teachers, policemen, or any other authority symbol in society.

3. Illusion

We live in a world of illusion, with people trying to impress each other. "One man pretends to be rich, yet has nothing; another pretends to be poor, yet has great wealth" (Prov. 13:7, NIV). Worth is measured by wealth, not by character and conduct; as long as people have money and fame, they're considered important. To be "rich and famous" is the ambition of millions of people; until they reach that goal, they enjoy riches and fame vicariously as they follow the career of their favorite celebrity.

Wise people believe God's truth and live for reality and not for illusion. "The wisdom of the prudent is to give thought to their ways, but the folly of fools is deception" (14:8, NIV). Some of the deceptive illusions people are foolishly clinging to today are:

"There are no consequences, so do as you please."
"If it feels good, it is good."
"The important thing in life is to have fun."
"There are no absolutes." (What about this statement?)
"The older generation can't teach you anything."
"Commitment is enslavement. Stay free."

Those of us who have had to counsel disillusioned people, some of whom were contemplating suicide, know how damaging these lies can be in the human life. A life that's built on lies is bound to be disappointing and will eventually fall apart. It's only when we build on God's truth that we can withstand the storms of life (Matt. 7:24-29).

To trust Jesus Christ is to know reality, because He is the truth (John 14:6). To know and obey God's Word is to know the truth (17:17), and to be empowered by the Holy Spirit is to experience truth (1 John 5:6). God is a God of truth, and those who know Him by faith have no desire to frolic in the senseless illusions of the world system (2:15-17).

4. Greed

"He who is greedy for gain troubles his own house" (Prov. 15:27, NKJV). "Hell and Destruction are never full; so the eyes of man are never satisfied" (27:20, NKJV).

A 1994 *Money* magazine survey indicates that Americans are a greedy lot and will even cheat to "make money." Twenty-four percent said they wouldn't correct a waiter who undercharged them, up from 15 percent in 1987; 9 percent said they'd keep money found in a wallet, up from 4 percent in their 1987 survey.[10] Here's the saddest of all: Twenty-three percent said they'd be willing to commit a crime to "get $10 million" if they knew they wouldn't get caught! The love of money is still a root of all kinds of evil (1 Tim. 6:10).

God calls covetousness idolatry (Eph. 5:5; Col. 3:5) because a covetous heart puts something else in the place that God rightfully should occupy in our lives. But the modern business society applauds covetousness and calls it "ambition" and "the first step to success." Business magazines praise the "pyramid climbers" who get to the top, no matter how they got there. Unfortunately, this contemporary view of success has invaded the church, and some Christian workers have thrown ethics and godliness aside in their quest to become important and successful.

An Arabian proverb says, "Covetousness has for its mother unlawful desire, for its daughter injustice, and for its friend violence." Is it any wonder that our modern covetous society witnesses so much injustice and violence? The only cure is to change the heart and replace desire for things with devotion to God, and only Jesus Christ can perform that miracle.

If believers today would read John Bunyan's *Pilgrim's Progress,* they'd meet Mr. Hold-the-World, Mr. Save-All, and Mr. Money-Love; they'd discover what Bunyan thought about Demas, the one-time associate of Paul who fell in love with "this present world" (Col. 4:14; Phile. 24; 2 Tim. 4:10). While it isn't a sin to be wealthy — Abraham and David were both wealthy men and yet godly men — it is a sin to want more than we really need and to keep what we ought to give. Covetousness is like cancer: It grows secretly and robs us of spiritual health, and the only remedy is to cut it out.

In chapter 7 of this book, we studied what Proverbs says about wealth, and there's no need to repeat it. The emphasis in Proverbs is on seeing material possessions as the gift of God, thanking Him for them, and using them for the glory of God and the good of others. John Wesley, founder of the Methodist Church, taught his people:

Do all the good you can,
By all the means you can,
In all the ways you can,
In all the places you can,
At all the times you can,
To all the people you can,
As long as you ever can.

If ever there was a prescription for curing greed, that's it!

5. Pride
Many theologians believe that pride is the "sin of all sins," for it was pride that changed an angel into the devil (Isa. 14:12-15). Lucifer's, "I will be like the Most High" (v. 14) challenged the very throne of God; in the Garden of Eden, it became, "You will be like God" (Gen. 3:5). Eve believed it, and you know the rest of the story. "Glory to man in the

highest" is the rallying cry of proud, godless humanity that's still defying God and trying to build heaven on earth (11:1-9; Rev. 18).

"The proud and arrogant man — 'Mocker' is his name; he behaves with overweening pride" (Prov. 21:24, NIV). "Before his downfall a man's heart is proud, but humility comes before honor" (18:12, NIV; see 29:23). God hates "a proud look" (6:16-17) and promises to destroy the house of the proud (15:25). Just about every Christian can quote Proverbs 16:18, but not all of us heed it: "Pride goes before destruction, and a haughty spirit before a fall" (NKJV).

The saintly Scottish preacher James Denney said, "No man can bear witness to Christ and to himself at the same time. No man can give the impression that he himself is clever and that Christ is mighty to save." That quotation should be printed in large letters and displayed in every church sanctuary and conference auditorium where God's people gather. It might humble some of the preachers and musicians who call so much attention to themselves that the hungry sheep can't see Jesus. If the greatest sin is the corruption of the highest good, then people who use the Christian religion to promote themselves are guilty of great transgression.

Solomon illustrated our desire for recognition and praise by writing about honey. "It is not good to eat much honey; so to seek one's own glory is not glory" (25:27, NKJV). Balance this with 25:16: "Have you found honey? Eat only as much as you need, lest you be filled with it and vomit" (25:16). If honey represents praise, then beware of trying to digest too much of it! More than one celebrity has admitted being "sick of it all" and wishing he or she could just enjoy life as a normal average citizen. I think it was the late radio comedian Fred Allen who defined celebrities as "people who work hard to be famous so they have to wear dark glasses so as not to be recognized."

"The pride of life" is one of the commodities that the world system offers (1 John 2:15-17), and most people will pay anything to acquire it. Bible commentator William Barclay said, "Pride is the ground in which all the other sins grow, and the parent from which all the other sins come." If we're going to get rid of the poisonous fruit, we have to attack the dangerous root; that's a painful thing to do. For the believer, the answer is found in obeying the Christ described in John 13:1-17 and Philippians 2:1-18.

The five "popular sins" I've discussed—drunkenness, disrespect, illusion, greed, and pride—have been with mankind since the days of the Flood, but for some reason, they seem to be even more prevalent today. Perhaps it's because the news coverage is better. Or maybe it's because we're in the last days. We expect to find these sins prevalent among lost people, but we don't expect to find them in the church. If the church ever hopes to witness to the lost world, it must be different from the lost world.

Paul learned that believers at Corinth were getting drunk at their church meetings (1 Cor. 11:21), and he warned them that drunkards would not inherit the kingdom of God (6:10; see 5:11).

Some children in the Ephesian church were not respecting and obeying their parents, and Paul reminded them that the Fifth Commandment still applied (Eph. 6:1-3).

The Apostle John warned the saints to whom he sent his first epistle that the world was passing away, with all of its illusions, and that they had better keep themselves from idols (1 John 2:15-17; 5:21).

Jesus warned His disciples, "Take heed, and beware of covetousness" (Luke 12:15); Paul wrote to the Colossian believers that covetousness was idolatry (Col. 3:5).

Paul cautioned the churches not to appoint young Christians to places of spiritual leadership, "lest being lifted up

with pride [they] fall into the condemnation of the devil"
(1 Tim. 3:6). And John had to deal with proud Diotrephes who
was running the church and wouldn't submit to the authority
of God's apostle (3 John 9-11).

Alas, these sins *are* found in the church!

James was right: "My brethren [and sisters], these things
ought not to be so" (James 3:10).

THIRTEEN

"This God Is Our God"

We study the Word of God so that we might better know the God of the Word. The better acquainted we are with God, the more we become like Him and acquire the skills we need for life and service. "The fear of the Lord is the beginning of wisdom, and the knowledge of the Holy One is understanding" (Prov. 9:10, NKJV). You can make a living without knowing many things, but you can't make a life without knowing God.

"It is impossible to keep our moral practices sound and our inward attitudes right while our idea of God is erroneous or inadequate," writes A.W. Tozer. "If we would bring back spiritual power to our lives, we must begin to think of God more nearly as He is."[1]

If we read the Book of Proverbs, or any book in the Bible, seeking only for doctrinal truth but ignoring God Himself, we'll miss what the Holy Spirit wants to say to us and do for us. It would be like a child devoting hours to studying the family album but not spending time with his family, getting to know them personally. If we have no growing acquaintance with God, then what we think we know about Him may be misleading; this hinders us from building a godly life. To quote Tozer again: "The essence of idolatry is the entertainment of thoughts about God that are unworthy of Him."[2] If that's true, and I believe it is, then it's possible to be a Bible student and also an idolater!

The Book of Proverbs reveals to us the wonderful God whom we should trust, obey, love, and get to know in a deeper way. As we grow in our intimacy with God, we will develop the wisdom and skills we need to be successful in making a life.

1. A holy God

According to Proverbs 9:10 and 30:3, God is "the Holy One"; the word translated "holy" means "utterly different, wholly other." God's very nature is holy: "You shall be holy, for I am holy" (Lev. 11:44-45; 19:2; 20:7, 26; 21:8, 15; 22:9, 16, 32; 1 Peter 1:16).[3] "God is light and in Him is no darkness at all" (1 John 1:5).

But we must not think of God's holiness simply as the absence of defilement, like a sterilized surgical instrument. Nor is God's holiness an inert, negative attribute. It's something positive and active, His perfect nature accomplishing His perfect will. It's like the "sea of glass mingled with fire" that John saw before the throne of God in heaven (Rev. 15:2). "For our God is a consuming fire" (Heb. 12:29; see Deut. 4:24).

Because He is holy, God hates sin (Prov. 6:17-19). Evangelists remind us that "God hates sin but He loves sinners," and certainly nobody will question God's love for a lost world (John 3:16; Rom. 5:8). But people can willfully sin so much that they become abominable to God. The perverse man is an abomination to God (Prov. 3:32; 11:20), and so are the proud (16:5), liars (12:22), cheats (11:1; 20:10, 23), hypocrites (15:8; 21:27; 28:9), and the unjust (17:15). Sin becomes so identified with the sinner that the very person becomes reprehensible to the Lord. This doesn't negate His love, but we must keep in mind that God's love is a *holy* love as well as a sacrificing love. It's a dangerous thing to play with sin and defy the living God. "He who is often rebuked, and hardens his neck, will suddenly be destroyed, and that without remedy" (29:1, NKJV).

Proverbs 21:12 calls God "the Righteous One" (NIV) or "the righteous God" (NKJV) and states that He judges the wicked for their wickedness. A holy God must be righteous in all His ways and just in all His dealings (24:11-12). "The curse of the Lord is on the house of the wicked, but He blesses the home of the just" (3:33, NKJV). Sometimes God sends immediate judgment on the wicked (2:22), but sometimes He merely takes away His restraining hand and allows the sinners' sins to judge them. "The evil deeds of a wicked man ensnare him; the cords of his sin hold him fast" (5:22, NIV; see Rom. 1:18ff).

2. A sovereign God

The fact that God is holy and just assures us that there are righteous principles that govern the universe and His dealings with us. As Dr. A.T. Pierson put it, "History is His story." "The Lord works out everything for His own ends — even the wicked for a day of disaster" (Prov. 16:4, NIV). "Many are the plans in a man's heart, but it is the Lord's purpose that prevails" (19:21, NIV). The Christian believer remembers Colossians 1:16: "All things were created by Him [Christ], and for Him." Jesus Christ is the Alpha and the Omega, the beginning and the end of all things.

The proud mind of sinful man rebels against the very thought of the sovereignty of God and affirms, "I am the master of my fate: I am the captain of my soul."[4] Charles Spurgeon said, "No doctrine in the whole Word of God has more excited the hatred of mankind than the truth of the absolute sovereignty of God. The fact that 'the Lord reigneth' is indisputable, and it is this fact that arouses the utmost opposition of the unrenewed human heart."[5]

Divine sovereignty doesn't destroy human responsibility and turn humans into robots. "To man belong the plans of the heart, but from the Lord comes the reply of the tongue" (16:1, NIV). "The lot is cast into the lap, but its every decision is from the Lord" (v. 33, NKJV). "A man's heart plans his way, but the Lord directs his steps" (v. 9, NKJV). God expects us to study, think, weigh possibilities, and make decisions, but we dare not "lean on [our] own understanding" (3:5). God promises to give wisdom to those who ask (James 1:5) and to direct those who are willing to obey (Prov. 3:5-6).

Because He is the Creator of all things, God is sovereign in nature (3:19-20; 8:22-31; 30:4). He's also sovereign in history and geography, controlling the rise and fall of rulers and nations (Acts 17:22-28; Dan. 4:17, 34-35). "By Me kings reign, and rulers decree justice" (Prov. 8:15). "The king's heart is in the hand of the Lord, like the rivers of water; He turns it wherever He wishes" (21:1, NKJV). "There is no wisdom or understanding or counsel against the Lord" (v. 30, NKJV).

Keep in mind that the God who decrees the end—His purposes—also decrees the means to the end. If He determines to overthrow Pharaoh and deliver Israel from Egypt, He also decrees that Moses and Aaron go to Egypt to confront Pharaoh. If He purposes to bring Israel into the Promised Land, He also decrees that Joshua shall be trained to lead them. If He purposes to win lost souls, He also decrees that a witness will share the Gospel. "And how shall they hear without a preacher? And how shall they preach unless they are sent?" (Rom. 10:14-15, NKJV)

The sovereignty of God is one of the greatest motivations for Christian life and service, because *we know that God is on the throne and controls all things.* His commandments are His enablements, and "we know that all things work together for good to those who love God, to those who are the called according to His purpose" (Rom. 8:28, NKJV). Instead of being a deterrent to evangelism, an understanding of divine sovereignty is a stimulus to biblical evangelism; for we are sure that God is "taking out" a "people for His name" (Acts 15:14, NKJV; see 18:1-11) and that His Word will not return void (Isa. 55:10-11). God is "not willing that any should perish" (2 Peter 3:9) but desires all people to be saved (1 Tim. 2:4), and Jesus commanded us to go into all the world with the message of salvation (Matt. 28:18-20). Our task is to obey and share the message; His responsibility is to save those who believe.

As sovereign Ruler over all things, the Lord sees and knows what's happening, the thoughts, actions, words, and motives of all people. "For a man's ways are in full view of the Lord, and He examines all his paths" (Prov. 5:21, NIV). "The eyes of the Lord are everywhere, keeping watch on the wicked and the good" (15:3, NIV). "The Lord weighs the hearts" (21:2, NKJV; see 17:3 and 24:12). When God judges, He judges justly, whether He's punishing the wicked or rewarding the righteous.

It's encouraging to know that "the Lord reigns" (Ps. 93:1) and that His righteous purposes will be fulfilled. Let's be sure that we're walking with Him on the path of life, surrendered to His will and seeking to honor His name.

3. A compassionate God

God's tender compassion and concern are seen in His care of the poor and needy. Widows and orphans in Israel were especially vulnerable to exploitation and abuse, and God warned His people in His Law to beware of mistreating them (Ex. 22:22; Deut. 10:18; 14:29; 26:12; 27:19).

"He who oppresses the poor reproaches his Maker, but he

who honors Him has mercy on the needy" (Prov. 14:31, NKJV; see 17:5). "The rich and the poor have this in common, the Lord is the maker of them all" (22:2, NKJV). When the Savior came to earth, He identified with the poor and the outcasts (Luke 4:16-21 2 Cor. 8:9), and God wants to show His compassion for them through His people. To harm the needy is to give pain to the heart of God.

"Do not rob the poor because he is poor, nor oppress the afflicted at the gate for the Lord will plead their cause, and plunder the soul of those who plunder them" (Prov. 22:22-23, NKJV). "The gate" was ancient Israel's equivalent of our modern courtroom, for there the elders met to settle village disputes. The poor might not be able to afford a lawyer, but God would come to their defense (23:10-11).[6]

Stealing the property of the poor was one way to get rich quick, even though the Law commanded that the ancient landmarks not be moved (22:28; Deut. 19:14; 27:17; Isa. 1:23; Hosea 5:10). God owned the land (Lev. 25:23) and loaned it to His people, and they were to keep their property within the tribes and clans. Family farms were marked off by stones, not fences; these ancient landmarks were to be honored and protected. "The Lord will destroy the house of the proud: but He will establish the border of the widow" (Prov. 15:25). The Lord keeps an eye on the property lines.

We can sin against the poor by neglect as well as by oppression. "Whoever shuts his ears to the cry of the poor will also cry himself and not be heard" (21:13, NKJV). "He who gives to the poor will not lack, but he who hides his eyes will have many curses" (28:27, NKJV). If we shut our ears and close our eyes, pretending to be ignorant of their plight, God will take note of it and shut His eyes to our needs and His ears to our prayers—and so will other people. We will reap what we sow. (See Deut. 15:7-11.)

"He who has pity on the poor lends to the Lord, and He

163

will pay back what he has given" (Prov. 19:17, NKJV). When we give to help others, we're actually giving to the Lord; He puts it on account and pays rich dividends (Phil. 4:15-17). "Inasmuch as you did it to one of the least of these My brethren, you did it to Me" (Matt. 25:40, NKJV). By the way, this principle also applies to the way we treat our enemies (Prov. 20:22; 25:21-22; Rom. 12:18-21).

God is a shield to those who trust Him (Prov. 30:5) and a strong tower for those who run to Him for help (18:10). "The name of the Lord" in verse 10 signifies all the glorious attributes of the Lord. Because of who He is and what He is, those who trust Him don't have to worry—because He is always their refuge and strength (Ps. 46:1).

One of God's compassionate ministries to us is that of *divine guidance.* Proverbs 3:5-6 is a promise God's people have been claiming for centuries, and it has never failed. As I said earlier in this book, God expects us to assess a situation and get all the facts we can, but we must never lean on our own understanding. We must humble ourselves before Him and seek His direction in all things, and we must be sure that our motives are right.

But what if we make a mistake, as we're all prone to do, and start to move in the wrong direction? "In his heart a man plans his course, but the Lord determines his steps" (16:9, NIV). "Many are the plans in a man's heart, but it is the Lord's purpose that prevails" (19:21, NIV; see 16:33). If we sincerely want to know and obey God's plan, the Lord will direct us and providentially guide our steps in ways that we may not understand. "A man's steps are of the Lord; how then can a man understand his own way?" (20:24, NKJV)

The Danish philosopher Sören Kierkegaard said, "Life can only be understood backward, but it must be lived forward." One day we shall look back and say with David, "Surely [only] goodness and mercy [have followed] me all the days of my life" (Ps. 23:6).[7] Knowing that God lovingly guides our steps as we seek to follow Him is a great encouragement when we don't know which way to go. "Who is the man that fears the Lord? Him shall He teach in the way He chooses" (25:12, NKJV). Even the great Apostle Paul wasn't always sure of the next step, but the Lord guided him (Acts 16:6-10).

4. A wise God

Theologians tell us that God's wisdom refers to His ability to devise perfect means to attain perfect ends. Nobody has to teach God anything. "For who has known the mind of the Lord? Or who has become His counselor?" (Rom. 11:34, NKJV; Isa. 40:13; Jer. 23:18). And nobody can ever say that God made a mistake, because in His wisdom, He does all things well (Rom. 8:28; 9:20-21). No wonder Paul called Him "God only wise" (16:27).

God has revealed His wisdom in creation. "By wisdom the Lord laid the earth's foundations, by understanding He set the heavens in place; by His knowledge the deeps were divided, and the clouds let drop the dew" (Prov. 3:19-20, NIV). The astronomer watching a comet through a telescope and the biologist peering at a cell through a microscope are both discovering God's wisdom, for scientific study is but the act of thinking God's thoughts after Him.

While seeking to witness to a university student whose religion was science, I noticed that he kept using the word "universe."

"Why do you say 'universe' and not 'multiverse'?" I asked.

Puzzled, the student said, "I don't understand what you mean."

"Well," I replied, "the word 'universe' implies that everything around us is one, a unity. If that's the case, where did this unity come from? What instituted the laws that you're studying in your science classes? Why do all these things work together and produce a 'universe' instead of a 'multiverse'?"

He saw which way the conversation was going and quickly changed the subject!

But my question is a valid one. If there weren't wisdom and order built into the universe (what most people call "scientific laws"), the farmer couldn't expect a harvest, the astronomer couldn't predict an eclipse, the scientist couldn't safely conduct an experiment, the pilot wouldn't be able to fly his plane, and nobody on earth would know from one moment to another what the stars and planets would do next! Isaac Watts said it perfectly:

I sing the wisdom that ordained
The sun to rule the day;
The moon shines full at His command,
And all the stars obey.[8]

God's wisdom is also seen in His *providential ordering of events,* not only for nations but also for individuals. "There is no wisdom, no insight, no plan that can succeed against the Lord" (21:30, NIV). "To God belong wisdom and power; counsel and understanding are His" (Job 12:13, NIV). The English word "providence" comes from the two Latin words *video,* "to see," and *pro,* "before." God in His wisdom "sees before," that is, plans in advance and "sees to it" that His will is accomplished.

Providence doesn't mean that God simply "foresees" what lies ahead and "adjusts" Himself accordingly. God alone knows and controls future events. The Baptist theologian Augustus Hopkins Strong calls providence, "that continuous agency of God by which he makes all the events of the physical and moral universe fulfill the original design with which he created it."[9] Without violating man's ability to choose, God "works all things according to the counsel of His will" (Eph. 1:11, NKJV) and rules and overrules in all things. "The Lord does whatever pleases Him, in the heavens and on the earth, in the seas and all their depths" (Ps. 135:6, NIV).

God wants to share His wisdom with us, which, of course, is the emphasis of the Book of Proverbs. "For the Lord gives wisdom; from His mouth come knowledge and understanding; He stores up sound wisdom for the upright" (2:6-7). *The first step in receiving God's wisdom is trusting Jesus Christ and becoming a child of God.* The world is frantically seeking the wisdom to know what to do and the power to be able to do it, and these are found only in Jesus Christ, "the power of God, and the wisdom of God" (1 Cor. 1:24).

The Gospel of salvation sounds like a foolish message to the lost world, for it seems foolish to commit your life to somebody who died on a cross in weakness and shame. But the preaching of that cross releases the power of God to change lives! (Rom. 1:16) "For the message of the cross is foolishness to those who are perishing, but to us who are being saved it is the power of God" (1 Cor. 1:18, NKJV).

After you trust Christ and become a child of God (John 1:11-13), the next step is to ask God to give you His wisdom in the ordering of your life (James 1:5). "The fear of the Lord teaches a man wisdom, and humility comes before honor" (Prov. 15:33, NIV). As you read His Word, meditate and pray, and seek to glorify Him, He will direct your steps (3:5-6). The way may not always be easy, but it will be the best way (Rom. 8:28). Remember that the will of God comes from the heart of God (Ps 33:11), so you don't have to worry.

When you have decisions to make, take time to pray and meditate on the Word. Ask God to direct you and, if necessary, seek wise counsel from friends who are mature in the faith. At the start of each day, ask God to guide you in every decision you must make, big or small; a wrong "small" decision could lead to disturbing "big" decisions. As you grow in the wisdom and knowledge of God, and as you walk by faith, seeking to honor the Lord, you will increase in spiritual discernment and live skillfully.

"The path of the righteous is like the first gleam of dawn, shining ever brighter till the full light of day. But the way of the wicked is like deep darkness; they do not know what makes them stumble" (Prov. 4:18-19, NIV).

To quote A.W. Tozer again: "With the goodness of God to desire our highest welfare, the wisdom of God to plan it, and the power of God to achieve it, what do we lack? Surely we are the most favored of all creatures."[10]

NOTES

Preface

1. T.S. Eliot, *Collected Poems 1909–1962* (New York: Harcourt Brace and World, 1963), 147.

Chapter One

1. There are also "wisdom psalms": 1, 19, 32, 34, 37, 49, 73, 78, 112, 119, 127–123, 133.

2. Roy Zuck, *Biblical Theology of the Old Testament* (Chicago: Moody, 1991), 232.

3. Among the Jews, proverbs were a popular and accepted way to digest and preserve wisdom. (For proverbs outside the Book of Proverbs see 1 Sam. 10:11-12; 24:13; Ezek. 12:22-23; 16:44; 18:1-2. See also Matt. 9:12, 17; 24:18; John 4:35, 37; 9:4; 1 Cor. 6:13; 14:8; 15:33.)

4. Proverbs 3:11-12 is quoted in Hebrews 12:5-6; 3:34 in James 4:6 and 1 Peter 5:5; 11:31 in 1 Peter 4:18; 25:21-22 in Romans 12:20; and 26:11 in 2 Peter 2:22.

5. Derek Kidner *Proverbs* in *Tyndale Old Testament Commentaries* (Downers Grove, Ill.: InterVarsity, 1964), 22.

6. Keep in mind that "wealth" means much more than possessing material things. The Bible doesn't promise that obedient Christians will all be healthy, wealthy, and successful. It does promise that they will have godly character, enjoy their Father's generous gifts to meet all their needs, and escape many of the physical and emotional pains and problems that the ungodly usually suffer. God's covenant with the Jews promised special blessings if they obeyed and chastisement if they disobeyed (see Deut. 27–28), but the Book of Proverbs also emphasizes the "true riches" of the spiritual life that are summarized in Christ's beatitudes. It has well been said that true happiness lies, not in the greatness of your possessions, but in the "fewness" of your wants.

7. Charles Bridges, *Exposition of the Book of Proverbs* (Grand Rapids: Zondervan, 1959), 3–4.

8. L.C. Harris, Gleason Archer, and Bruce Watke, *Theological*

Wordbook of the Old Testament, vol. 1 (Chicago: Moody, 1980), 283.

9. The phrase, "the beginning of the creation of God" in Revelation 3:14 (KJV) cannot mean that Jesus was the first thing God created, since the Son of God was with the Father before there was a creation (John 1:1-5). The Greek word *arche* can mean either "first in time" or "first in rank"; therefore the NIV translates the phrase, "the ruler of God's creation." The familiar title, "firstborn" can also refer to rank. As "the firstborn of every creature" (Col. 1:15, KJV), Jesus is the head of creation ("the firstborn over all creation," NIV).

10. Remember that the Hebrew society was strongly masculine and that primarily the fathers trained the sons while the mothers trained the daughters. The masculine emphasis in Scripture must not be interpreted as a sexist bias but rather as a characteristic of the Jewish culture of that day, a characteristic that should no longer persist in the light of the Gospel (Gal. 3:26-29).

11. The Hebrew word for *hear* is *shema.* The Jewish confession of faith in Deuteronomy 6:4-5 is called "The Shema." Implied in the word "hear" is receiving and obeying God's Word.

12. Andrew A. Bonar, *Memoir and Remains of Robert Murray M'Cheyne* (London: Banner of Truth, 1966), 29.

Chapter 2

1. The father's statement, "my son," is found forty-one times in Proverbs, but the influence of the mother isn't ignored. See 1:8; 4:3; 6:20; 10:1; 15:20; 19:26; 20:20; 23:22; 23:25; 28:24; 30:11, 17; 31:1ff.

2. James 1:14 uses the images of hunting and fishing to get the same point across. The verbs "drawn away" and "enticed" carry the idea of "luring with bait," whether baiting a trap or a fishing hook. Temptation is the bait, and Satan wants us to think we can grab the bait and avoid the consequences (Gen. 3:5). Alas, it never works that way.

3. In Proverbs, three Hebrew words are translated "fool": *kesyl,* the dull, stupid fool; *ewiyl,* the corrupt fool who is morally pervert-

ed; *nabal,* the stubborn, brutish fool whose mind is made up and won't be convinced. For a vivid example of this third variety of fool, see 1 Samuel 25.

Chapter 3

1. This has been my life verse since 1948 when I entered seminary to prepare for ministry, and I can bear witness that it has never failed me. When you walk on God's path, you delight in God's presence and enjoy God's pleasures. You have life, joy, and pleasure — and it gets better and better as life progresses!

Chapter 4

1. I realize that modern psychology considers to be "sexual" many if not most of our human responses to one another; for, after all, we are sexual beings and not robots. However, the phrase "sexual intimacy outside the bonds of marriage" refers specifically to intercourse and forms of sexual relationship that substitute for intercourse. Our Lord spoke of "fornications" (plural) in Matthew 15:19; the edict of the Jerusalem conference mentioned "fornication," which certainly included the sexual sins condemned by the Law of Moses (Acts 15:20; Lev. 18). It appears that in some contexts the words "adultery" and "fornication" are inclusive of various forms of sexual sins.

2. Quentin Crisp wrote this in *Manners from Heaven,* chapter 7.

3. *The Myth of the Greener Grass,* by J. Allan Petersen (Wheaton, Ill.: Tyndale, 1983), is one of the best books from a biblical point of view on understanding and preventing extramarital affairs and healing marriages that have been violated by them. As every pastor knows, more of this kind of sin goes on in local churches than we dare openly admit.

4. The basic meaning of the Hebrew word is "to go astray, to err" and can describe the results of drinking too much alcohol (20:1; Isa. 28:7). It's translated "go astray" in Proverbs 5:23 (KJV); in verses

19-20, it means "to be ravished, intoxicated."

5. The command to bind God's Word to various parts of the body was taken literally by the Pharisees (3:3; 6:21; 7:3; Deut. 6:8-9); this was the origin of the "phylactery" (Matt. 23:5), a small leather case containing four portions of the Old Testament (Ex. 13:1-10 and 11-16, and Deut. 6:4-9 and 11:13-21) written on parchment. When attending public prayers, the orthodox Jew tied one phylactery to his forehead and the other to his left arm. They also put a phylactery at the door of their house. "Phylactery" is a word that comes from the Greek and means "to watch over, to safeguard." It was their belief that wearing God's Word like an amulet would protect them from evil.

Chapter 5

1. Let me remind you that the Book of Proverbs has a definite masculine focus because in the ancient Jewish society daughters usually weren't educated for the affairs of life. Most of them were kept secluded and prepared for marriage and motherhood. For the most part, when you read "man" in Proverbs, interpret it generically and read "person," whether male or female. Proverbs isn't a sexist book, but it was written in the context of a strongly male-oriented society.

2. George Morrison, *Sunrise: Addresses from a City Pulpit* (London: Hodder and Stoughton, 1903), 169–77. Kregel Publications has embarked on the project of reprinting all of George Morrison's books, and I recommend them to you. He was a peerless preacher.

3. Some contemporary theology so emphasizes God's love that it loses sight of the fact that God also hates. God has no pleasure in sin (Ps. 5:4). Sin grieves the Father (Gen. 6:6), the Son (Mark 3:5), and the Spirit (Eph. 4:30). Love and hatred can exist in the same heart (see Ps. 97:10, Amos 5:14-15, Ps. 45:7, and Rom. 12:9). If God's people loved holiness more, they would hate sin more. God is love (1 John 4:8, 16), but He is also light (1 John 1:5) and a consuming fire (Heb. 12:29).

NOTES

Chapter 6

1. Charles R. Bridges, *Exposition of the Book of Proverbs* (Grand Rapids: Zondervan, 1959), 179.

2. Brooks Atkinson, *Once around the Sun* (New York: Harcourt, Brace, 1951), 37.

3. This oft-quoted statement is the last line of Thomas Gray's poem, "Ode on a Distant Prospect of Eton College," but its message is usually misunderstood. In the poem, Gray contrasts the joyful innocence of children in school to the difficulties they will have when they reach adulthood. He asks us not to rob them of their youthful pleasures too soon. There will be time enough for them to learn that life isn't always fun and games. We expect a certain amount of naive innocence in children, but not in adults.

4. Ralph Waldo Emerson, *Essays: First and Second Series* (New York: E.P. Dutton, 1938), 31. Emerson was one of the preachers of the "success philosophy" that has become the unofficial civil religion of the United States. His essay, "Self-Reliance," is the "Bible" of the under-believers and overachievers in the business world, and some of its humanistic ideas have infiltrated the church and produced a "success theology" that is unbiblical. I enjoy reading Emerson, but I carefully separate the wheat from the chaff.

5. There is a "sanctified self-confidence" that's based on faith, energized by the Holy Spirit, and glorifies God. Paul expressed it when he wrote, "I can do all things through Christ who strengthens me" (Phil. 4:13, NKJV); David gave testimony to it in Psalm 18:29-39.

6. Isaac's favoritism toward Esau (Gen. 25:28), Jacob's pampering of Joseph (Gen. 37:3), and David's failure to discipline his sons properly all helped to create the family problems I've mentioned.

7. Some commentators translate the phrase "drink violence" ("damage") as "to be stripped bare." In other words, send a fool on an important mission and you'll end up crippled and humiliated!

Chapter 7

1. The origin of the word 'scam' is obscure. It comes from carnival jargon and may be a variation of the word "scheme." Before the

law stepped in to control such things, some carnival workers were notorious at fleecing the unsuspecting public with get-rich-quick offers. Alas, what was once confined to carnivals is now found on Wall Street.

2. Of course, we don't give to others in order to get something back, because that would be selfish. We must be motivated by love and a desire to honor the Lord.

3. The story of "King Midas and the Golden Touch" is supposed to teach this important lesson. As the king acquired more and more gold, he discovered the hard way the things that were really important to him.

4. I wrote that in jest, of course, but only to get your attention and remind you of your accountability before God. Christians will want their last will and testament also to be a last will and *testimony*. How we dispose of the wealth God gives us, whether it be little or much, tells other people what is really important to us. It's frightening how many professed believers don't even have a will! Where is their sense of stewardship?

Chapter 8

1. In marriage, two people become one flesh (Gen. 2:24); therefore, if one partner dies, the marriage is dissolved (Rom. 7:1-3) and the living partner may remarry "in the Lord" (1 Cor. 7:39). The Book of Proverbs doesn't whitewash the problems that can be faced in marriage, but nowhere does it deal with divorce. It magnifies God's original plan for marriage and the home, and that's what we should do today. People who get married with one hand on an escape hatch aren't likely to have a happy home.

2. Jesus makes it clear in Matthew 19:11-12 that not everybody is supposed to get married, and Paul states that singleness is a gift from God just as much as is marriage (1 Cor. 7:7). I once heard the gifted Christian educator Henrietta Mears say that the only reason she wasn't married was because the Apostle Paul was dead!

3. The proverb, "Spare the rod and spoil the child" goes back to the days of Rome *(Qui parcit virge, odit filium* = "Who spares the

rod, hates [his] son") and has been in English literature since the year 1000. Those exact words aren't found in Scripture, but Proverbs 13:24 comes closest: "He that spareth his rod hateth his son: but he that loveth him chasteneth him betimes [early]." The Roman proverb no doubt comes from the Hebrew proverb, which is much older.

4. In *The New American Commentary*, Duane A. Garrett translates the verse, "Train up a child in a manner befitting a child, and even as he grows old he will not turn from it" (Nashville: Broadman Press, 1993), vol. 14, 188. See also Gleason Archer's explanation in *The Encyclopedia of Bible Difficulties* (Grand Rapids: Zondervan, 1982), 252–53. We don't know how much spiritual instruction Solomon received from his father David, but when Solomon was old, he turned away from the Lord (1 Kings 11:1-8). Some students think that Ecclesiastes is his "confession of faith," written after he returned to the Lord, but the book doesn't say so and it isn't wise to speculate.

Chapter 9

1. Robert B. Downs, *Books That Changed the World* (New York: New American Library, 1956), 129.

2. Steven Pinker, *The Language Instinct* (New York: William Morrow, 1994), 15, 18. Dr. Pinker is professor and director of the Center for Cognitive Neuroscience at the Massachusetts Institute of Technology. In his book *The Difference of Man and the Difference It Makes*, philosopher Mortimer J. Adler calls human speech "the pivotal fact." He says that "man is the only talking, the only naming, declaring or questioning, affirming or denying, the only arguing, agreeing or disagreeing, the only discursive, animal" (New York: World Publishing Co., 1968), 112. That is what makes us different from the "other animals."

3. According to Genesis 3:1-7, Satan tempted Eve to eat of the forbidden tree so she would become like God, "knowing good and evil." But it isn't necessary to disobey God to develop discernment; His divine wisdom instructs us concerning good and evil, and is our "tree of life" (See Prov. 3:18).

4. The Greek word translated "sound" *(hugiaino)* gives us the English word "hygiene," and means, "to be sound in health."

5. The Hebrew word translated "quarrel" has legal overtones and can refer to a lawsuit (Ex. 23:2-3, NIV). Solomon's counsel is wise: it's better to keep cool and speak calmly than to argue with your opponent and end up with an expensive lawsuit that nobody really wins.

6. The Greek word translated "willing to yield" ("easy to be entreated") speaks of a conciliatory attitude and not a compromising bargain that seeks for "peace at any price." Conciliatory people are willing to hear all sides of a matter and honestly seek for areas of agreement. They are open to "yielding to persuasion." Some people mistake prejudice and stubbornness for conviction and faithfulness.

7. In his novel *Nineteen Eighty-Four,* George Orwell warned us about "newspeak"; in his book *Double-Speak* (New York: Harper & Row, 1989), William Lutz explains today's version of what Orwell predicted half a century ago. It's frightening!

Chapter 10

1. Paul is referring to Abraham's faith in Genesis 15:6. Some people have the idea that sinners during the Old Testament era were saved by good works while sinners today are saved by faith in Christ, but this idea is wrong. *Anybody who has ever been saved has been saved by faith, because nobody can be saved by good works (Eph. 2:8-9).* Hebrews 11 informs us that Old Testament saints were saved by faith, and Habakkuk 2:4 states, "The just shall live by his faith." This verse is quoted in Romans 1:17, Galatians 3:11, and Hebrews 10:38; these three epistles make it very clear that salvation is by faith in Jesus Christ and faith alone.

2. Justification is the gracious act of God whereby He *declares* the believing sinner righteous in Jesus Christ and gives us a righteous standing in His sight. Sanctification is the divine process whereby God *makes* His children more like Jesus Christ as we walk in the Spirit and yield to His will. The person who is justified will want to

reject sin and obey God because justification involves sharing the life of God as well as having a right standing before God (Rom. 5:18). A right position before the Lord leads to a right practice in daily life.

Chapter 11

1. God never violates any person's freedom, but He works so that His purposes are accomplished even through the lives of people who don't know Him or won't acknowledge Him. This was true of Cyrus (2 Chron. 36:22; Isa. 44:28–45:1), Nebuchadnezzar (Jer. 25:9; 27:6), and Pharaoh (Ex. 9:16; Rom. 9:14-18).

2. The KJV reads "A man who hath friends must show himself friendly" and the margin of the NKJV reads "A man who has friends may come to ruin." The idea seems to be that having many companions *but no real friends* could lead a person to ruin, for there's nobody who cares enough about him to rebuke him. The original text is difficult, but the NIV seems to say it best.

3. Psalm 46:10 says, "Be still, and know that I am God"; the phrase "be still" literally means "take your hands off," or "stop your striving." There are times when we prove our faith simply by waiting on the Lord and allowing Him to work. Naomi's advice to Ruth was excellent: "Sit still, my daughter" (Ruth 3:18), and so was Moses' instruction to Israel at the Red Sea: "Stand still!" (Ex. 14:13) But when it's time to act, no amount of devotion will substitute for obedience. See Joshua 7:10ff, 1 Samuel 16:1ff, and 1 Kings 19:15ff.

4. *The Westminster Pulpit*, vol. IV (London: Pickering and Inglis), 147.

Chapter 12

1. Arnold M. Washton and Donna Boundy, *Willpower's Not Enough* (New York: Harper & Row, 1989), 7–18.

2. See Habakkuk 2:15; Isaiah 5:11-22; 28:1-3; Amos 6:3-6; Deuteronomy 21:20.

3. I haven't been able to learn when the Jews added wine to their Passover meal, although some authorities claim the custom goes back to the days of the first temple. Wine isn't mentioned in Exodus 12:11-27, but by the time you get to the New Testament, wine is a part of the meal (Matt. 26:26-30). Would they use unleavened bread and leavened (fermented) wine? Since four different cups of wine were used in the ceremony, the wine was diluted.

4. *The Lincoln (Neb.) Star,* July 15, 1994.

5. It's worth noting that immorality is closely associated with drunkenness (Prov. 23:27-28), for the two often go together.

6. The Hebrew word translated "redness" in the KJV and "bloodshot" in the NIV, means "dullness, dimness." The drunkard's vision is blurred so that he doesn't see clearly what is there and claims he sees what isn't there. Too much alcohol can produce bloodshot eyes as well as a ruddy face. Some expositors think that the word suggests "blacked eyes," i.e., as the result of a fight; yet true as it is, that probably isn't what the writer had in mind.

7. Lemuel means "devoted to God" and may have been another name for King Solomon. God's special name for Solomon was Jedidiah, which means "beloved of Jehovah." We don't know for sure who King Lemuel and his mother were and it's useless to speculate.

8. In Paul's day, wine was used for medicinal purposes (1 Tim. 5:23), but this doesn't give us license to make an ancient practice into a modern norm. Many people seize this one verse but reject everything else Paul wrote in this epistle. If we're going to obey one admonition, why not obey all of them?

9. A report issued by the Commission on Substance Abuse at Colleges and Universities, sponsored by Columbia University, states that drinking is a serious problem on American campuses. Ninety-five percent of violent crime on campus is alcohol-related. Sixty percent of the female students who had sexually transmitted diseases were "under the influence of alcohol at the time of intercourse," and alcohol was involved in 90 percent of all campus rapes. At the time of the survey, 42 percent of the students (men and women) admitted "binge drinking" within the previous two weeks. One-third of the students drink primarily to get drunk. Students

NOTES

who live in fraternity and sorority houses drink more than other students. One ponders the future of the nation if the next generation of leaders is already suffering from "bottle fatigue."

10. Twenty-one percent of the people ages eighteen to thirty-four would keep the money, but only 2 percent of the people sixty-five and older would do so. Where is our younger generation getting its ethical standards?

Chapter 13

1. A.W. Tozer, *The Knowledge of the Holy* (New York: Harper and Brothers, 1961), 7. This is one of the finest devotional studies of the attributes of God in print. See also Richard L. Strauss, *The Joy of Knowing God* (Neptune, N.J.: Loizeaux, 1984).

2. Ibid., 11.

3. For a fuller treatment of the subject, see *Be Holy*, my exposition of Leviticus (Wheaton, Ill.: Victor Books, 1994).

4. The quotation is from "Invictus" by William Ernest Henley. The word *invictus* is Latin for "invincible, unconquered." Henley suffered from tuberculosis of the bones and bravely endured at least twenty operations, but one wishes he had given the Lord credit for some of the determination that kept him going. We admire any person's courage in the face of seeming defeat, and his poem is an inspiring clarion call to personal courage, but the Christian believer would prefer 2 Corinthians 12:7-10.

5. These were the opening words of his sermon preached at the Metropolitan Tabernacle, London, on Sunday evening, February 4, 1866. See vol. 58 of *The Metropolitan Tabernacle Pulpit*, 13.

6. The word translated "redeemer" in Proverbs 23:11 is *goel* and refers to the kinsman-redeemer, such as Boaz in the Book of Ruth. For the law governing the redemption of property, see Leviticus 25:47-55. The *goel* had to be a close relative who was willing to pay and able to pay. He is a picture of Jesus Christ, who in His incarnation took upon Himself flesh and blood (Heb. 2:14) that He might redeem us from our spiritual bankruptcy and sin. See my book *Be Committed* for an exposition of Ruth and an explanation of the law of the kinsman-redeemer.

7. Most scholars believe that Psalm 23 was a product of David's latter years and not the poem of a young shepherd. It's possible that it grew out of the insurrection caused by his wicked son Absalom (2 Sam. 15–19). David had experienced many difficulties in his long life, yet he saw only God's goodness and mercy.

8. The hymn we call, "I Sing the Mighty Power of God," Isaac Watts entitled, "Praise for Creation and Providence." It was originally written for children. For some reason, we've lost one verse from some of our hymnals:

His hand is my perpetual guard,
He guides me with His eye;
Why should I then forget the Lord,
Whose love is ever nigh?

Paul used divine creation as part of his proof that the Gentiles, who were never given the revelation God's Law, are still guilty before God and will be judged by Him (Rom. 1:18ff).

9. A.H. Strong, *Systematic Theology,* one-volume edition (Philadelphia: The Judson Press, 1949), 419. Strong goes on to say, "Providence does not exclude, but rather implies the operation of natural law, by which we mean God's regular way of working. . . . Prayer without the use of means is an insult to God" (p. 439).

10. Tozer, *The Knowledge of the Holy,* 70.

Chapter One

Don't Just Make a Living—Make a Life!

1. How has the Holy Spirit functioned as a "spiritual radar" in your life?

2. What is the difference between being smart and being wise? Give your own definition of what it means to be "spiritually wise"?

3. Describe a person you have known who was "spiritually wise."

4. How does knowing God more help us to be wiser?

5. If, as Wiersbe says, being wise is like a skill, how do we work at being wiser?

6. What do you understand "the fear of the Lord" to mean?

7. How does fearing God make us wiser?

8. Why do think the proverbs in this book cover a variety of topics?

9. Give some examples of how wisdom makes a difference in our day-to-day lives.

Chapter Two

Is Anybody Listening?

1. What noises in our world distract our attention from God?

2. If you were comparing "wisdom" and "folly" to two modern women, how would they each be dressed?

3. One of the voices that speaks in Proverbs is the voice of instruction. Who has been a voice of instruction in your life?

4. Another voice that speaks in Proverbs is the voice of temptation. How would you describe the sound of the voice of temptation? What kind of wealth do we receive from wisdom?

5. In what ways does hearing God's truth always demand that we make a choice?

6. What kind of labels would we use today to describe the "scorners" (those people who have rejected God's truth and even disdained it)?

7. What would be the difference between someone who rejects God's truth out of scorn and someone who rejects God's truth out of foolishness?

8. Proverbs teaches us that wisdom and folly are both calling out to us, and we must make a choice to follow one or the other. Describe the difference between what wisdom and folly call to us to do.

9. What makes it difficult to follow the voice of wisdom even when we know it is the right thing to do?

Chapter Three

The Path of Wisdom and Life

1. In thinking of our lives as a journey, what kind of road would you say you've spent most of your life traveling on?

2. How do we walk differently when we walk in wisdom?

3. List some ways that wisdom protects our path.

4. Give an example of how making wise choices has helped you find the right direction in your life?

5. Explain how the definition "to lie helpless, facedown" is an accurate description of what it means to trust God?

6. Describe how we show our trust in God when we share our blessings?

7. How does living according to God' wisdom make us view our world differently?

8. How does understanding the world through God's wisdom affect what comes out of our mouths?

9. How does God's wisdom affect what we see ahead of us?

10. Describe the difference between a path created by folly and a path created by wisdom.

Chapter Four

The Path of Folly and Death

1. Describe the benefits of being sexually pure.

2. What are some reasons that sexual sin is taken so lightly in much of our society?

3. How does a casual view of sex lead to disappointment and disillusionment?

4. What kind of logic drives people to a life of casual sexual encounters even though they know they will be disillusioned?

5. In what ways does sexual sin eventually destroy us?

6. How is adultery like stealing?

7. Why is purity often looked down on in our culture?

9. What are the differences and similarities between the dangers of premarital sex and adultery?

10. How does God's wisdom help us to remain sexually pure?

11. How does remaining sexually pure help us to seek God's wisdom?

Chapter Five

People, Wise and Otherwise—Part 1 (The Wise & the Wicked)

1. If the wisest thing anyone can do is trust Christ, then why are there such intelligent people who have never made the decision to follow Christ?

2. What keeps us from listening to instruction or advice?

3. Wiersbe writes: "Wise people don't waste their time listening to foolishness and lies." What kinds of foolishness and lies do we need to avoid in our world today?

4. How do we show our fear of God (the beginning of wisdom) in our everyday choices?

5. Explain how our own wisdom can be affected by keeping company with fools or people who lack wisdom? And is the opposite true?

6. In what ways does wisdom affect our speech?

7. Think of a time when the wisest choice was to run rather than trust yourself not to sin. In light of that situation, respond to this statement: "The wiser you are, the easier it should be not to sin."

8. In listening to someone talk, what tells you whether he is wise or wicked?

9. Describe the difference between a wise and wicked person in the way they deal with conflict within a group of people.

Chapter Six

People, Wise and Otherwise—Part 2 (The Simple, Scorner, and Fool)

1. What is the difference between the kind of faith we put in God and the kind of faith we put in people?

2. What is the danger of being simple, or naïve?

3. How can the fear of God make a simple person wiser?

4. What kind of humility does it take to become wise?

5. What is the danger of being a scorner, in other words, unteachable?

6. How can the fear of God make a scorner wiser?

7. In your opinion, why does a fool talk "big" but never follow through?

8. In what ways does the confidence of a fool keep him from gaining wisdom?

9. What would you say is the best advice for a simple person, scorner, or fool?

Chapter Seven

"Rich Man, Poor Man, Beggar Man, Thief"

1. Describe the latest get-rich-quick scheme that you've heard about.

2. When does laid-back turn into lazy?

3. What are the consequences for a sluggard and those involved with him?

4. List some ways that being lazy is like being a thief.

5. What kinds of things do thieves steal from us besides our money?

6. Sometimes poverty is created by tragic situations and sometimes by foolish habits. What are some of the foolish lifestyle choices that create poverty?

7. Describe our basic struggle in knowing how to help the poor.

8. What is our responsibility, if any, to those who have less than us?

9. Read Proverbs 4:23. What are some ways in which God is honored when we live diligent lives?

10. How does debt relate to greed?

Chapter Eight

Family, Friends, and Neighbors

1. Think of someone who you would consider to have poor people skills. What are some of the problems he or she faces?

2. How do the three institutions God created (family/home, government, local church) interrelate and influence each other?

3. Name some of the responsibilities that husbands and wives have, in regards to their marriage, that require wisdom.

4. Read Proverbs 31:10-30 aloud a few verses at a time. Then restate after each few verses, in modern terms, the characteristics of a godly woman.

5. In the days of the Old Testament, children were seen as blessings. What words or phrases would best describe how children are seen today.

6. In light of the wisdom of Proverbs, what should children learn from their parents?

7. How does the discipline of a child affect what he learns about wisdom?

8. In what ways does disciplining our children reflect the way we discipline ourselves?

9. List some guidelines for when to be "brutally honest" with a friend and when to be gentle.

10. Name some ways that wisdom makes each of us a better friend and family member.

Chapter Nine

A Matter of Life or Death (Human Speech)

1. Think of the most powerful words you've ever heard (positive or negative, public or private). Describe what made them so powerful.

2. Read aloud Proverbs 25:11-12. What similarities do you see between our words and fine jewelry?

3. Read aloud Proverbs 15:1. Describe a time when you saw a gentle answer in action.

4. For those of us who acknowledge the power of God in our lives, why are we still sometimes careless with our words?

5. List some ways we help others with our words.

6. What are some of the ways lying affects relationships?

7. From your experience, name some of the dangers of gossip.

8. What are some of the best ways you have found to keep your angry words under control when you are arguing with someone?

9. Name some of the dangers of the kind of speech we refer to as "talking off the top of my head," or "thinking out loud."

10. What are the best arguments for using as few words as possible?

Chapter Ten

Make Way for the Righteous!

1. What kind of person do you think of when you hear the word *righteous?*

2. What kind of righteousness do you hope or expect to see in yourself?

3. In what ways does our righteousness grant us deliverance?

4. What is the difference between "righteousness" and "self-righteousness"?

5. How is having good character like or unlike having righteousness?

6. How does our own righteousness affect our family life?

7. List some unrighteous activities that our society has come to accept as "OK." (hints: cheating on taxes, speeding, little white lies, etc.)

8. In Old Testament days the righteousness of a king determined the righteousness of a nation. What kind of correlation can you see between those days and our national leadership today?

9. Wiersbe states: "The church collectively and believers individually aren't doing their job in spreading righteousness." How should we be spreading righteousness?

10. Read 2 Chronicles 7:14. How can the truth of this verse help us find the kind of righteousness described in Proverbs?

Chapter Eleven

Enjoying God's Guidance

1. How do you define the "will of God"?

2. Read Proverbs 3:5-6. According to these verses, explain in your own words how we receive guidance from God.

3. When we go through difficult times, what makes it difficult to believe that God has our best interests at heart?

4. What part does waiting play in understanding God's will?

5. In what ways can being "cafeteria Christians" (picking and choosing what parts of God's will we want to accept) cause us to miss out on some of the best parts of God's will?

6. Read Proverbs 16:9. What does this Scripture teach us in regard to detours and regrets that we face in life?

7. Think of the people who you go to for wise counsel. What kind of qualities causes you to trust them to help you determine God's will in your specific situation?

8. Read Proverbs 19:21. What kind of comfort can we take from this Scripture?

9. Describe the balance between taking responsibility for acting out our own plans and giving God room to guide us in our plans.

10. What part does our obedience play in God's freedom to reveal His will to us?

Chapter Twelve

Popular Sins (Drunkenness, Disrespect, Illusion, Greed, Pride)

1. Wiersbe alludes to the role that the media plays in our sensitivity to sins such as drunkenness, disrespect, and greed. How would you describe the role that the media plays?

2. How does alcohol affect our ability to act wisely?

3. Why is the abuse of alcohol so prevalent in our culture?

4. In what ways does the abuse of alcohol keep us from helping ourselves?

5. Proverbs has a lot to say about a younger generation showing respect for the older generation. How does our nation measure up to this standard set in Proverbs?

6. In the Old Testament days the punishment for a child's rebellion was death. What would that kind of severity accomplish in our culture?

7. Name some illusions you grew up believing that became disappointments in your adult life.

8. Read Proverbs 15:27. What examples of greed have you seen around you lately?

9. Proverbs gives many warnings about a proud heart. What are the dangers of pride?

10. What would be your diagnosis of why these sins (drunkenness, disrespect, illusion, greed, and pride) often seem just as prevalent inside the church as they do outside of it?

Chapter Thirteen

"This God Is Our God"

1. Proverbs teaches us of a God who is holy. How does Proverbs teach us to be like God?

2. Read Proverbs 8:15. What does this short verse teach us about God's sovereignty?

3. What kind of comfort do you find for your day-to-day life in the fact that God is in control of this world?

4. Read Proverbs 19:17. What does this verse teach us about God's compassion?

5. What kinds of things stand in our way as we seek to be compassionate like God is compassionate?

6. In what ways do you see God's wisdom revealed in creation?

7. In what ways do you see God's wisdom revealed in Christ's sacrifice for us?

8. If you could put the message of Proverbs, the book of wisdom, into one sentence, what would it be?

9. What are the earmarks of a person who is growing in wisdom?

10. List some of the changes a foolish person needs to make in order to become wise?